THE

FA
TROPHY

PAUL EADE

TEMPUS

By the same author

Scarborough Football Club (Images of Sport), Tempus Publishing, 2002
Workington Association Football Club (Images of Sport), Tempus Publishing, 2003

First published 2004

Tempus Publishing Ltd
The Mill, Brimscombe Port
Stroud, Gloucestershire GL5 2QG
www.tempus-publishing.com

British Library Cataloguing in Publication Data.
A catalogue record for this book is available from the British Library.

ISBN 0 7524 2941 8

Typesetting and origination by Tempus Publishing.
Printed and bound in Great Britain

Contents

Acknowledgements

Acknowledgements are due to the following for all their invaluable help and assistance in compiling this book. In particular, I must give special thanks to professional photographer Paul Dennis, for providing, free of charge, the vast majority of images from the finals of the 1990s. Thanks also go to: Doreen Benford/*The Shropshire Star*, Jim Whitton (Barrow), Roger Slater (Wealdstone), Charles Place/*The Scarborough Evening News*, Ali Kazemi (Kingstonian), Jen Tombs/Woking FC, Ron Duggins, Don Hale, *The Matlock Mercury*, *The North-West Evening Mail*, Dave McLean/*The Staffordshire Newsletter*, Howard Nurse/BBC Sport online, Stan Strickland/Burscough FC, Ian C. Walmsley (Canvey Island), The Football Club History Database, Leek Town FC, Morecambe FC, Bangor FC historical website, Mossleyweb (http://kickme.to/mossleyweb), Bishop's Stortford FC, all the staff at Tempus Publishing, plus anybody else who helped in any way.

Introduction

The FA Trophy has been non-League's premier cup competition since its inception in 1969. Many look upon it as the successor to the FA Amateur Cup, but, in fact, the hugely successful latter competition ran alongside the trophy before its last final in 1974. The trophy was created because it was felt that clubs with professional players who could only enter the FA Cup should have a more realistic chance of making it to play in a Wembley final. Following the demise of the Amateur Cup, the FA Vase was introduced the following season. That format has continued ever since, with teams from the top two levels of the National Leagues system (the FA Conference and its three feeders, the Northern Premier, the Southern and the Isthmian Premier Division and Division One only), competing in the FA Trophy and those below that level invited into the FA Vase.

The trophy quickly established itself as the most important cup competition for clubs outside the Football League. While an FA Cup run could bring a lot of national exposure and the chance for some giant-killing, the trophy was a winnable competition offering many players and fans a chance they would otherwise never experience – to represent their side in a Wembley final.

Entries for the first trophy competition in 1969/70 included eight clubs who were destined to enter the Football League: Barnet, Cambridge United, Hereford United, Kidderminster Harriers, Macclesfield Town, Scarborough, Wimbledon and Wigan Athletic. Macclesfield beat Telford United 2-0 in the first final, watched by 28,000 at Wembley.

The competition quickly gained popularity, with attendances for the finals well in excess of 20,000, and there was a 'golden era' in the early 1990s when Wycombe Wanderers and Colchester United ensured three successive finals with attendances easily topping 30,000 – the crowd of 34,842 in 1991 being a competition record.

The competition suffered something of a body blow after 2000, with the closure of Wembley. A final under the Twin Towers had been the primary pulling point of the trophy and to play at Villa Park, while still being special, could never have quite the same grandeur. In addition, clubs' increasing concerns over finances led the trophy to take a back seat for some, with an FA Cup run offering greater monetary reward.

That said, an attendance of 18,809 for the 2002 final between Yeovil Town and Stevenage Borough showed that the competition was still very much alive and kicking. Yeovil won the trophy on the road to promotion to the Football League the following season and the competition has seen seven winners, plus another three clubs that have appeared as losing finalists, going on to League membership.

That trend was established from the start, with Macclesfield Town meeting Telford United in the inaugural final, with Macclesfield winning 2-0. Telford returned the following year to beat Hillingdon Borough 3-2, the first of three final victories for the club. Only Scarborough and Woking can match that tally, though Telford hold the record for the total number of appearances in a final at five. Telford are thus, arguably, the most successful trophy side of all time, especially as their performances have been spread out over a number of years, while for Scarborough and Woking the glory years came in a clutch, which seems quite a common phenomenon, with teams often reappearing in the final in a short space of time. Stafford Rangers won the trophy twice and were runners-up once in the space of seven years in the 1970s. Altrincham visited Wembley in 1982 and 1986 and Kidderminster reached the final in 1987, and again in 1991. The 1991 winners Wycombe Wanderers returned in 1993 to beat Runcorn, the latter the only team to lose in the final in successive seasons.

The trophy has also seen a good slice of its own romance and giant-killing, in non-League terms. Mossley performed wonders to reach the final in 1980, while in 1989/90 Leek Town, in the Northern Premier League Division One at the time, beat holders Telford, former winners Stafford Rangers and Conference Champions-in-waiting Darlington, before finally being beaten 3-0 by Barrow in the final. But the biggest fairytale came in 2002/03, when Unibond League Burscough, normally used to quietly playing in front of 230 fans, sensationally knocked out Conference Champions Yeovil before beating Dr Martens League Champions Tamworth in front of 14,265 spectators at Villa Park.

The trophy continues to thrive, with 205 entries for 2003/04. The competition currently starts with the preliminary round in October and runs through to the final in May with a £50,000 prize for the winners.

Paul Eade
April 2004

1970

Macclesfield Town 2, Telford United 0
Wembley, 2 May 1970

Macclesfield Town lived up to their reputation as the toughest side in non-League football by overpowering Telford United to win the inaugural FA Trophy final. Dave Lyon and Brian Fidler grabbed the goals as the Silkmen shrugged off intense heat in front of 28,000 spectators at Wembley. Victory was no more than Macclesfield deserved. They had earned the status of one of the best non-League teams in the country after reaching the FA Cup third round in 1967/68, followed by winning the Northern Premier League title in its first season in 1968/69, a championship that they retained shortly after this cup triumph.

Macclesfield's league and cup double was testimony to the managerial skills of Frank Beaumont. The former Bury, Barnsley and Stockport County player instilled a hard-work ethic into his small squad, leading by example on the pitch, and his method paid dividends. Beaumont knew that Telford United, under the player-management of former England international Ron Flowers, would be no pushover. With former Wolves forward Jimmy Murray – an FA Cup winner with his former club in 1960 – plus former Northern Ireland international goalkeeper Bobby Irvine in their side, Southern Leaguers Telford had a touch of class.

Indeed, it was Telford who started brightly, with Flowers pulling the strings in midfield. In the twenty-fourth minute Telford nearly snatched the lead when left-back Geoff Croft's lob was tipped over by Macclesfield 'keeper John Cooke. A minute later, Macclesfield were in front. Winger Merrick Corfield showed why he had won several players' awards by opening up Telford's defence down the right. His hard, low pass was controlled by Dick Young, who set up Lyon to shoot past three defenders and Irvine. Lyon said, 'Dick Young pushed a short pass to me and yelled "hit it". It went beautifully into the corner of the net. I felt like rushing out of the ground to tell my mother at home!'

Telford had their best chance to level just after the start of the second half. Telford's leading scorer Jack Bentley powerfully headed Flowers' cross. The ball beat Cooke, but John Bennett somehow got himself in the way before Cooke gratefully grasped the ball right on the goal line.

That seemed to spur Macclesfield into action and Brian Fidler's pace began to cause problems for Telford. Meanwhile, Macclesfield's tremendous work rate kept Telford's attackers at bay, no more so than when Beaumont cleared off the line from Brian Hart.

Fidler put the game beyond doubt on sixty minutes. Sent clear by David Lyon and with Telford's defenders appealing vainly for offside, Brian Fidler only had Irvine to beat and, as the 'keeper rushed out in a desperate attempt to keep him at bay, Fidler launched a lob from thirty yards that dropped just inside the post.

Club showman Brian Fidler sprinted eighty yards, hurdled the perimeter fence and stood triumphantly on the greyhound track to acknowledge the Maxonians' cheers. 'I was on my way to collect my medal', Fidler later joked. 'Supporters pay to be entertained and if my running round makes them happy, it makes me very happy.'

Still Telford refused to throw in the towel and Cooke had to be at his very best when diving at full stretch to his right to keep out a goal-bound shot from Micky Fudge. But gaps opened in Telford's defence as they threw caution to the wind and Brian Fidler, his unrelated team-mate Dennis Fidler and Lyon all went close for Macclesfield. Beaumont urged his tired players through the closing minutes by telling them, 'If you think you're tired, took at Telford – and they haven't got a goal for their pains.' When the final whistle came, Beaumont was reduced to tears. He said, 'I was in some joyous trance. It was the greatest moment of my life when I lifted that trophy.'

Flowers was understandably dejected, but said: 'Macclesfield took their chances well and John Cooke was picking up everything in goal. I congratulate Macclesfield on their win.' Flowers was a magnificent leader, but Macclesfield were a side that seemed to have no limits. Two days later, they turned out again to win the North-West Floodlit League Trophy at Witton, and then on Thursday travelled to Scarborough to win a nail-biting championship decider 1-0 in front of a 6,031 crowd at the Athletic Ground. This must be something to note down for professionals today who complain of being asked to play 'too many' games!

Macclesfield Town: Cooke, Sievwright, Bennett, Beaumont, Collins, Roberts, Lyon, B. Fidler, Young, Corfield, D. Fidler. Substitute: Berry.

Telford United: Irvine, Harris, Croft, Flowers, Coton, Ray, Fudge, Hart, Bentley, Murray, Jagger. Substitute: Ball.

Above: Macclesfield goalkeeper John Cooke gets down to save from Telford winger George Jagger.

Right: Macclesfield's programme for 1970/71 illustrated one of the winning Wembley goals on the front cover.

In Focus
Telford on the Map

Despite losing at Wembley, Telford's appearance in the 1970 final was a significant step for the club. Until then, the name of Telford United was not widely known, even in football circles. That was because the name Telford United only came into being in 1969, when the New Town of Telford was designated. Previously the same club was known as Wellington Town, with a history dating back to 1872.

Wellington had proved a successful club in non-League circles, winning the championship of the Birmingham League in 1921, 1935 and 1936, before moving on to the Cheshire League, which they won three times after the Second World War. Wellington joined the Southern League (North-Western Section) in 1958 and in that season qualified for founder membership of the Premier Division.

However, it was with the renaming of the club to Telford, and the expansion of the area with New Town status, that Telford United began to make further headway. In 1971 they were back for a second FA Trophy final and this time emerged as 3-2 victors over Hillingdon Borough, in a season that also saw them win the Southern League.

Telford were one of the founder members of the Alliance Premier League in 1979 and have remained in non-League's top flight ever since, cementing their ever-increasing reputation with memorable performances in both the FA Trophy and FA Cup. In 1982/83 Telford appeared in their third FA Trophy final at Wembley and gained a 2-1 victory over Northwich Victoria. A string of FA Cup runs followed, with Stockport County, Northampton and Rochdale put to the sword in 1983/84 and the fifth round reached in 1984/85 with a visit to Everton, where Telford were defeated 3-0 but far from disgraced.

The 1987/88 and 1988/89 seasons saw Telford reach successive trophy finals, losing to Enfield after a replay at The Hawthorns and gaining a single-goal victory over Macclesfield to gain revenge for their defeat in the first final.

Routes to the Final

Macclesfield Town

First round	Macclesfield Town 1, Burscough 0
Second round	Macclesfield Town 2, Gainsborough Trinity 0
Third round	Bangor City 1, Macclesfield Town 1
Third-round replay	Macclesfield Town 1, Bangor City 0
Fourth round	Burton Albion 1, Macclesfield Town 1
Fourth-round replay	Macclesfield Town 4, Burton Albion 2
Semi-final (at Stoke City)	Macclesfield Town 1, Barnet 0

Telford United

Third qualifying round	Telford United 5, Witton Albion 0
First round	Ilkeston Town 0, Telford United 2
Second round	Telford United 1, Wigan Athletic 0
Third round	Romford 1, Telford United 1
Third-round replay	Telford United 2, Romford 1
Fourth round	Worcester City 1, Telford United 3
Semi-final (at Swindon)	Telford United 2, Chelmsford City 0

1971

Telford United 3, Hillingdon Borough 2
Wembley, 1 May 1971

In 1971, Telford United put the previous year's disappointment behind them by returning to Wembley to lift the FA Trophy. Telford's Micky Fudge kept up his record of scoring in every round by netting the eighty-sixth-minute winner that earned Telford a 3-2 victory. Hillingdon, who went in at half-time 2-0 up and thinking that the trophy was theirs, were worn down by Telford's comeback and looked a tired side when Fudge grabbed the winner. Fudge and Joey Owen combined to find a gap in the Hillingdon defence and, with goalkeeper Mick Lowe lured off his line, Fudge shot accurately to claim his tenth FA Trophy goal of the season.

The finale was a sharp contrast to the first forty-five minutes, when Hillingdon looked much the sharper side. Telford's normal passing game was absent and it was no surprise when Hillingdon took the lead in the seventeenth minute. Johnny Bishop, a find for Hillingdon from local football, put in a measured cross that striker Eddie Reeve glanced into the goal with his head.

Telford looked shell-shocked, and two minutes before half-time Bishop showed why he had been attracting the attention of Football League scouts with a delightful chip over Bobby Irvine. Disgusted Telford coach Ron Flowers gave his side an interval roasting and told them to start moving the ball about Wembley's wide pitch. But Telford still needed a swift goal to get back into the game – and it came in the fifty-third minute.

Defender Geoff Croft won the ball for Telford and picked out top scorer Joe Owen. Owen showed why he had scored 41 goals during the season by eluding Vic Batt's challenge and firing an unstoppable shot to make it 42 and put Telford back in the hunt.

Telford's tails were suddenly up and Hillingdon were pushed harder and harder as they desperately tried to defend their slim advantage. But that evaporated on eighty-one minutes, when a three-man move involving George Jagger, Paul Coton and Fudge found the head of leading scorer Jack Bentley, who made no mistake with a well-directed header.

Hillingdon looked visibly shattered and it was no surprise five minutes later when Fudge made the trophy Telford's. A delighted Flowers said:

> I thought I was watching a tennis match in the first half. We never looked like playing and Hillingdon deserved their lead. But I could still see us coming back provided that we settled down and pushed the ball about. The early goal in the second half put us back in with a chance and we took it.

Telford captain Graham Carr admitted that it was Flowers who had engineered the fightback. 'In the first half we were terrible and everybody's head was hanging in the dressing room,' he said. 'But Ron told us to play the ball about when we got it and his advice worked wonders. I must give credit to Ron for that talk. He told us to play football and he was right.'

Hillingdon player-manager Jim Langley took the defeat philosophically. At forty-two, he was the oldest player to appear in a cup final at Wembley. Indeed, he had played for England against Portugal at Wembley back in 1958 and in 1967 was a member of the victorious Queen's Park Rangers team that defeated West Bromwich Albion 3-2 to win the League Cup. He admitted, 'Telford deserved their win and it could not happen to a nicer bloke than Ron Flowers.'

A curious footnote to the game was the return of Telford's club flag, borrowed by a supporter for the game. The flag was taken from its pole during the week before the game and an anonymous caller telephoned *The Shropshire Star* newspaper to say that it had been borrowed and would be returned after the final. When Telford's players were about to go into the dressing room after their lap of honour, a fan called over Graham Carr, and, saying 'here's your flag back,' thrust the missing item into the Telford skipper's arms. It couldn't have been returned more promptly!

Telford United: Irvine, Harris, Croft, Ray, Coton, Carr, Fudge, Owen, Bentley, Jagger, Murray. Substitute: Hart.

Hillingdon Borough: Lowe, Batt, Langley, Higginson, Newcombe, Moore, Fairchild, Bishop, Reeve, Carter, Knox. Substitute: Vafiadis.

Johnny Ray (with cup) and Geoff Croft parade the FA Trophy after Telford's great fightback to beat Hillingdon Borough.

In Focus
The Rise and Fall of Hillingdon Borough

'Hillingdon aim for Cup glory and League status', read a feature in the 1971 FA Trophy final match programme. How times change. Nowadays, you would be hard-pressed to find Hillingdon's results, as they ply their trade in the Spartan South Midlands League at the tiny Middlesex Stadium in Ruislip. In 1971 it was a different story. Hillingdon were a stable Southern League club with their sights set firmly on the Football League. They had good claims, too. Financially sound, Hillingdon owned their 20,000 capacity Leas Stadium with covered accommodation for 6,000 and modern facilities. A record gate of 9,033 was achieved in 1969 when Hillingdon beat Luton Town 2-1 in the second round of the FA Cup, only to fall to fellow non-Leaguers Sutton United in the next round.

The following year Hillingdon made their first bid for election to the Football League but gained no votes as Cambridge United got entry. Hillingdon tried again a year later on the back of their FA Trophy final appearance, but again did not receive a vote. Hillingdon's fortunes subsequently took a dive and they were relegated from the Southern League Premier Division in 1973/74, but bounced back after one season and in 1978/79 only narrowly missed the cut for entry into the new Alliance Premier League.

Failure to join non-League's elite spelled the beginning of the end for Hillingdon Borough. Following a financial crisis the club was wound up after the 1983/84 season and Leas Stadium was sold.

The club did not die completely, however, as a merger with Burnham saw the creation of Burnham and Hillingdon FC. But this soon proved to be just a vehicle to allow Burnham to take Hillingdon's place higher up the pyramid and, in 1987, the name Hillingdon was dropped from the club title.

The year 1997 saw the re-emergence of Hillingdon Borough in the Spartan South Midlands League, where they have attained a series of mid-table placings. A far cry, however, from Wembley 1971.

Routes to the Final

Telford United

First round	Telford United 6, Bradford Park Avenue 1
Second round	Telford United 7, South Shields 1
Third round	Burton Albion 0, Telford United 2
Fourth round	Tamworth 1, Telford United 1
Fourth-round replay	Telford United 6, Tamworth 1
Semi-final (at West Bromwich)	Telford United 3, Yeovil 1

Hillingdon Borough

First round	Hillingdon Borough 3, Corby Town 1
Second round	Chelmsford City 1, Hillingdon Borough 2
Third round	Wigan Athletic 0, Hillingdon Borough 1
Fourth round	Hillingdon Borough 2, Buxton 0
Semi-final (at Leicester)	Hillingdon Borough 2, Hereford United 0

1972

Stafford Rangers 3, Barnet 0
Wembley, 15 April 1972

After ninety-six years of waiting, Stafford Rangers collected the first major cup in the club's history in 1972, when they defeated Barnet to bring the FA Trophy back to Marston Road. Three tremendous goals in a dazzling seven-minute spell in the second half sealed victory for Stafford and left Barnet a broken side.

Much of the credit for the second-half domination of Stafford Rangers was due to wingers Gerry Jones and Mike Cullerton, who responded to manager Roy Chapman's half-time advice to 'get in behind the full-backs' with deadly precision. They had a hand in all three goals. The first half, however, was close, with both sides enduring their own moments of pressure, though Rangers always looked more dangerous in front of goal. Barnet's main threat came from highly rated winger Colin Powell, but he wasted his speedy breaks down the right with indifferent finishing.

Just before half-time, Stafford's top scorer Ray Williams gave a warning of what was to come, leaving two men in his wake before hitting a low drive just past the far post.

The second half belonged almost exclusively to Stafford, with Barnet's former Arsenal goalkeeper Jack McClelland constantly being called into action. Spurred on by their supporters, who made up around seventy-five per cent of the 24,000 crowd, Rangers smoothly eased up through the gears into overdrive.

The first goal came in the sixty-fifth minute and was a perfect example of effective simplicity in football. Cullerton's cross-field ball found striker Gerry Jones, and the ladies hairdressing salon owner crossed to the far post, where Terry Bailey nodded it back for Williams to volley the ball into the back of the net. Six minutes later Cullerton, a cousin of Arsenal's Peter Marinello, made it 2-0. The forward broke through on the right to latch on to a touch pass from Bailey and thunder an unstoppable drive past McClelland.

Left: Graham Chadwick holds the FA Trophy high after Stafford Rangers' 3-0 victory over Barnet.

Right: Roy Chapman, Stafford's manager in 1972, who would go on to lead Rangers to Wembley on two further occasions.

Before Stafford's jubilant fans had sat down, they were celebrating again. Jones crossed to the far post and there was Williams ghosting through to head down past a surprised McClelland. It was his forty-third goal of the season and equalled the club's scoring record. The closing fifteen minutes allowed Rangers to turn on the style, notably when midfield dynamo Stuart Chapman sold a beautiful dummy that had the crowd roaring for more. Rangers returned to Stafford on Sunday afternoon to a welcome of 20,000 people lining the streets. The team, in a coach with the trophy, travelled to the town centre via the Marston Road ground.

Then, on Monday, before 5,575 spectators – the largest gate of the season – Rangers ran round the pitch with the trophy and then slipped seamlessly back into action to beat Bradford Park Avenue 3-2.

Stafford Rangers: Aleksic, Chadwick, Clayton, Sargeant, Aston, Machin, Cullerton, Bailey, Williams, Chapman, Jones. Substitute: Barlow.

Barnet: McClelland, Lye, Jenkins, Ward, Embery, King, Powell, Ferry, Flatt, Eason, Plume. Substitute: Adams.

In Focus
Rangers Rise from the Depths

From the brink of bankruptcy and extinction, Stafford Rangers rose in just six years to become one of the most powerful sides outside the Football League in 1972. Yet in 1966, Rangers had twice applied for re-election to the Cheshire League and had rarely finished far away from the bottom of the table for the previous fourteen years. Only a tote draw run by their most loyal fans kept the club on its feet.

Colin Hutchinson, appointed manager in 1965, slowly turned things around and the 1967/68 season saw a change of fortune. Rangers finished ninth in the league and defeated Runcorn to win the Cheshire League Cup. Twelve months later, the club finished runners-up to Skelmersdale. Crowds had rocketed from 200-300 to 2,000 and entry was gained to the newly formed Northern Premier League.

Rangers' first campaign in the Northern Premier League (1969/70) saw them finish in seventh position and win the Midland Floodlit Cup. In the summer of 1970, Colin Hutchinson left, to be replaced by player-manager Roy Chapman. This marked the beginning of the most successful spell in the club's history. Chapman, who scored a hat-trick on his Stafford debut, brought all the experience of a career with Aston Villa, Lincoln, Mansfield, Chester and Port Vale with him and with this a new professionalism flourished at the club.

In 1970/71, the team got off to a great start with just one defeat in the first 22 league games, including a remarkable 7-5 win at Great Harwood. On 26 December 1971, Rangers topped the table with a 4-point lead over Wigan Athletic, who had also only suffered one defeat. The top two met at Wigan, but in front of a crowd of 8,107 Rangers lost by a single goal. In the return fixture at Easter, a record attendance of 6,501 gathered at Marston Road but Wigan won 1-0 and Rangers had to settle for the runners-up spot.

In 1971/72 Rangers completed a treble of the Northern Premier League Championship, the FA Trophy and the Staffordshire Senior Cup, with Ray Williams scoring a club record of 48 goals. After Chapman departed to manage Stockport County, Rangers were again at Wembley in 1975/76 for their second FA Trophy final, but they lost to Scarborough 3-2 after extra time, in a season when they were just pipped to the Northern Premier League title by Runcorn.

Chapman returned for a second stint and took Stafford to a second FA Trophy final success in 1979, this time against Kettering Town, and Rangers became one of the founder members of the Alliance Premier League.

Routes to the Final

Stafford Rangers

Preliminary round	Rhyl 0, Stafford Rangers 1
First round	Bradford Park Avenue 1, Stafford Rangers 1
First-round replay	Stafford Rangers 1, Bradford Park Avenue 0
Second round	Stafford Rangers 3, Ilkeston 0
Third round	Hillingdon Borough 1, Stafford Rangers 2
Fourth round	Stafford Rangers 1, Macclesfield Town 1
Fourth-round replay	Macclesfield Town 0, Stafford Rangers 3
Semi-final (at Oxford)	Yeovil Town 0, Stafford Rangers 4

Barnet

First round	Dover 0, Barnet 6
Second round	Lowestoft 0, Barnet 0
Second-round replay	Barnet 5, Lowestoft 0
Third round	Wigan Athletic 1, Barnet 2
Fourth round	Dartford 0, Barnet 2
Semi-final (at Northampton)	Barnet 1, Telford United 0

1973

Scarborough 2, Wigan Athletic 1
Wembley, 28 April 1973

Scarborough showed tremendous reserves to finally overcome Wigan Athletic with a decisive goal deep into extra time. Boro thought they had the game wrapped up after leading for most of normal time, but had to pick themselves up after Wigan snatched an equaliser with just thirty seconds left on the clock.

Wigan went into the match as favourites, with 16,000 supporters in the 23,000-strong crowd on the fiftieth anniversary to the day of the 1923 FA Cup final, the first game played at Wembley Stadium. But it was Scarborough who settled into the game the better and they took the lead on twelve minutes. A Gerry Donoghue cross was not properly cleared and Malcolm Leask was on hand to crack the ball past Wigan goalkeeper Dennis Reeves. It was only the second goal that Reeves had conceded during the season's competition.

Wigan fought back, and Graham Oates, who had scored in all but one of the previous trophy rounds, shot wide from a Paul Clements cross before Bernie Fagan headed away to deny John Rogers. Then giant Scarborough 'keeper, Bert Garrow, threw his sixteen-stone, 6ft 3in frame to turn a Mick Worswick effort round the post.

Scarborough had their moments, though, and Donoghue brought the best out of Reeves with a stinging shot. Boro player-manager Colin Appleton marshalled his side well and as they pushed forward, Reeves had to cut out a series of crosses. Just before half-time the game swung back towards Wigan, as Garrow fisted away under pressure and Appleton headed a cross away. Wigan pushed for an equaliser after the interval, but found Garrow commanding his area. Scarborough began to counter-attack and it took a clearance from former Arsenal trainee Ian Gillibrand to stop Leask from reaching a pass from Boro veteran Alan Franks.

Wigan had a penalty appeal turned down when a shot from Oates hit Dick Hewitt and the decision seemed to put the Latics on the back foot. With Gerry Donoghue taking charge in midfield for Boro, Malcolm Thompson headed wide and Reeves caught a George Siddle header.

On seventy-three minutes Boro brought on Jeff Barmby to replace Leask and the ever-dangerous frontman soon found himself in the clear only for Reeves to save at his feet. Reeves again stopped a Barmby dribble and, with the seconds ticking away, the Boro fans were happily whistling for the end of the game. But Wigan youngster John Rogers hit his fifteenth goal of the season when he hammered a volley through a crowded goalmouth following a Boro scramble to clear.

With rain pouring down, both sides looked leg-weary in extra time, though Boro were inches away when Thompson headed on a free-kick from Scarborough captain Jimmy Shoulder. A replay at Bramall Lane looked to be on the cards, but in the twenty-sixth minute of extra time Harry Dunn played a through ball to Thompson, who chested it down, rounded a defender and smacked the ball past Reeves as he came out to narrow the angle.

There was no second comeback for Wigan, as Garrow cut out a high cross from Wigan captain Albert Jackson before the final whistle went, and Boro's fans celebrated to the tune of 'Oh I do Like to Be Beside the Seaside.'

Of the winning goal, Thompson reflected, 'Maybe it was not the greatest goal I have ever scored, but certainly it was the most important of my life.' A delighted, exhausted Appleton said:

> For so long we have had to work hard and even to the death, today we had to work hard for our success. In the past our luck has gone against us, and for once it has not. We knew how long the game had to go and then Wigan got their equaliser. Then we had to pick ourselves up again. It says a great deal for the character of the side that we did.

Scarborough: Garrow, Appleton, Shoulder, Dunn, Siddle, Fagan, Donoghue, Franks, Leask, Thompson, Hewitt. Substitute: Barmby.

Wigan Athletic: Reeves, Morris, Sutherland, Taylor, Jackson, Gillibrand, Clements, Oates, Rogers, King, Worswick. Substitute: McCunnell.

In Focus
Appleton's Crowning Glory

Scarborough's first FA Trophy success was the culmination of four years of progress under Colin Appleton. Appleton, born in Scarborough in 1936, made his debut for Boro in 1951/52, only to be snapped up by Leicester City, first appearing for the Foxes in March 1954. He went on to make 328 first-team appearances for Leicester, captaining them in their 1963 FA Cup final defeat against Manchester United, and after leaving Leicester in 1966 he was captain at Division Two side Charlton Athletic.

Left: Scarborough player-manager Colin Appleton holds the FA Trophy.

Right: Colin Appleton kisses the FA Trophy in one last pose for the cameras as the crowds drift away from Wembley.

Appleton then enjoyed a successful spell at Barrow before coming home to join Scarborough as player–manager in the summer of 1969. His arrival ranks as one of the most significant appointments in the history of Scarborough Football Club. His dedication to detail and thorough professionalism quickly paid dividends and he quickly transformed the team from a run-of-the-mill non-League side to consistent championship challengers in the Northern Premier League.

During 1969/70 Scarborough were transformed into a major force, winning 20 league matches, including an 8-0 trouncing of Great Harwood, with Jeff Barmby, a diminutive striker recently signed from Goole Town, netting four goals. A run of six successive wins saw Boro involved in a thrilling climax to the season, with four clubs chasing the championship. Boro joined Macclesfield Town, Wigan Athletic and Boston United in a close battle at the top of the table, and on Thursday 7 May, reigning champions Macclesfield visited the Athletic Ground.

It was Boro's last match of the season, and victory would have given them the championship. A few days earlier Macclesfield had become the first ever winners of the FA Trophy, and a crowd of 6,031 assembled at the Athletic Ground for what had become a virtual championship decider. The visitors won by a single goal to retain their title on goal average from Wigan Athletic, leaving Boro in fourth position, just 2 points behind the champions. In fact, a new era had begun, with Colin Appleton turning Boro into one of the top sides in non-League football. Scarborough finished third and fourth in the Northern Premier League in the 1970/71 and 1971/72 seasons respectively, before the 1972/73 term saw the beginning of the Wembley glory years.

Appleton found the final pieces of the jigsaw, with giant goalkeeper Bert Garrow and striker Malcolm Leask both arriving from South Shields. Boro finished second in the Northern Premier League, but it was the FA Trophy victory that really brought the club to the attention of the whole town and a wider football audience.

Appleton left Boro in a healthy state when he left to become coach at Grimsby Town in November 1973 and his long-term replacement was eventually named as Ken Houghton. Houghton took Boro back to Wembley in 1975, where they lost 4-0 to Matlock, but Appleton returned as manager in the summer following his dismissal at Grimsby. Under Appleton's second tenure Scarborough made Wembley a second home, with further final victories in 1976 and 1977, and also became founder members of the Alliance Premier League in 1979.

Appleton finally left in 1981, going on to manage Hull City, and his impact at Scarborough cannot be overstated. A consistently winning, professionally run team, FA Cup runs, but above all the string of FA Trophy glories massively raised their standing and meant that, for the first time, League football became a serious and consistent ambition for the club. That the latter aim was realised in 1987 was in no small part due to the foundations laid by Appleton, without whom Scarborough may never have held such lofty aims.

Routes to the Final

Scarborough

First round	Scarborough 3, Macclesfield Town 1
Second round	Sandbach Ramblers 0, Scarborough 3
Third round	Mexborough Town 1, Scarborough 3
Fourth round	Scarborough 2, Chelmsford City 0
Semi-final (at Peterborough)	Scarborough 1, Ashford Town 0

Wigan Athletic

First round	Wigan Athletic 5, Burton Albion 0
Second round	Wigan Athletic 2, South Liverpool 0
Third round	Wigan Athletic 2, Romford 0
Fourth round	Morecambe 1, Wigan Athletic 1
Fourth-round replay	Wigan Athletic 0, Morecambe 0
Fourth round, second replay (at Blackburn)	Wigan Athletic 1, Morecambe 0
Semi-final (at Port Vale)	Wigan Athletic 0, Stafford Rangers 0
Semi-final replay (at Oldham)	Wigan Athletic 1, Stafford Rangers 0

1974

Morecambe 2, Dartford 1
Wembley, 27 April 1974

Two brilliant goals in the space of two minutes sealed FA Trophy glory for Morecambe at the expense of odds-on favourites Dartford. Dartford were 4-7 with the bookies to take the trophy as they won the Southern League by 8 clear points, while Morecambe were seventeenth in the Northern Premier League. But, once again, it was the southern-based team that went home disappointed.

After a steady first twenty minutes, in which both sides showed their willing-ness to attack, the game suddenly moved into top gear. Morecambe striker Tony Webber latched onto a long clearance, progressed down the right and crossed the ball along the ground for Malcolm Richmond, whose shot struck Dartford 'keeper John Morton's body but still went into the net. The Morecambe fans' jubilation had not even subsided before Morecambe were two up. Again Webber picked up the ball on the right, this time trying a shot himself that struck Dartford defender Graham Carr and fell to Jimmy Sutton, who shot accurately and strongly into the roof of the net.

Morecambe's supporters were soon chanting, 'we want three', and Webber almost obliged with a shot that Morton saved at the foot of the post. Dartford were in disarray, especially defending the flanks, where Webber was having a field day. But, on forty minutes, Dartford went agonisingly close to pulling one back, Keith Robinson's shot hitting the upright. This seemed to give Dartford the impetus they had previously lacked and just before half-time Morecambe player-manager Dave Roberts cleared off the line, following a Ken Halliday cross.

But Morecambe regained their composure after the interval and Morton was soon at full stretch to once again stop a Webber shot in the shadow of the post. Roberts was a constant thorn in Dartford's side and he won a corner that put Dartford's defence in a tangle, before Morton eventually gathered.

As time wore on Dartford had to commit to attack and it looked as if the game would soon slip further away from them as Morecambe exploited their increased space to roam the Wembley turf. Webber again set himself up for a shot that beat Morton but, to the Man of the Match's disbelief, the ball struck the bar before Richmond was narrowly unable to capitalise on the rebound.

Dartford refused to give up and Morecambe began to visibly tire, with eighteen-year-old Keith Galley coming on for Roberts, who was suffering from cramp. Galley was far from overawed and embarked on several probing runs with the ball but Dartford began to enjoy more possession.

In the last ten minutes it was all Dartford, with Morecambe 'keeper John Coates the busiest man on the pitch, but it was not until injury time that Dartford got a goal, Dave Cunningham finding enough space in the box to drive the ball home from a point near the penalty spot. Dartford urgently placed the ball back on the centre spot, but Morecambe managed to close out the last few seconds in the middle of the park before the final whistle signalled a mini pitch invasion from a section of Morecambe's younger supporters.

Roberts, a member of the Macclesfield team that won the FA Trophy in 1970, had passed on to his side a confidence that the trophy would be theirs. Even after Morecambe had won at Mexborough in the first round, he told the local press that the Shrimps were on their way to Wembley. After Morecambe had triumphed, he explained:

> I had no doubts we would win the trophy. Just because we are lowly placed in the Northern Premier League does not mean we are a bad side.... Our fourteen-man pool was ideal for a good cup run and I was so glad we played Dartford in the final. Our league champions Boston might have beaten us but I do not think the Southern League teams rate as highly and our victory confirms northern superiority in non-League soccer.... I told the lads at half-time not to relax. We had played them off the park but could not afford to relax our grip. We didn't and Dartford had no real chance of making a fightback.

Morecambe: Coates, Pearson, Bennett, Sutton, Street, Baldwin, Done, Webber, Roberts, Kershaw, Richmond. Substitute: Galley.

Dartford: Morton, Read, Payne, Carr, Burns, Binks, Light, Glazier, Robinson, Cunningham, Halliday. Substitute: Hearn.

In Focus
Morecambe's Finest Hour

(Reproduced with thanks from Morecambe FC's official website)
Saturday 27 April 1974 is a date forever embroidered in the rich tapestry that is Morecambe's history. A 2-1 victory over Dartford, with goals by Malcolm Richmond and Jimmy Sutton, with over 9,000 Shrimps supporters in a crowd of

over 19,000, is the merest of the recorded statistics. However, the day belonged to Morecambe, in what was arguably the club's finest hour.

The path to Wembley was a difficult and traumatic one. After a comfortable 3–0 victory at Mexborough, old rivals Bangor City were overcome 2–1 at Christie Park. Kettering Town, with Ron Atkinson, came to Christie Park and held the Shrimps to a 0–0 draw. Kettering, giants of the non-League world at that time, felt – and said as much in the press – that the job was done, that victory for the Poppies at Rockingham Road was a foregone conclusion. Somebody forgot to tell Morecambe, who put on a magnificent display, winning the game 2–1. Tony Webber, a schoolteacher, who scored the two goals, taught Kettering an important lesson that night: never count your chickens.

Above: Morecambe FC 1973/74. From left to right, back row: Geoff Street, Dave Roberts (player-manager), Dave Pearson, John Coates, Barrie Kershaw, Bob Baldwin (captain).
Front row: Malcolm Richmond, Keith Galley, Tony Webber, Stephen Done, John Bennett, Jim Sutton.

Right: Official programme for the 1974 FA Trophy final.

F.A. CHALLENGE TROPHY COMPETITION

FINAL

DARTFORD

VERSUS

MORECAMBE

SATURDAY, 27th APRIL, 1974   Kick-off 3 p.m.

WEMBLEY

STADIUM

OFFICIAL PROGRAMME 10p

Another non-League giant, Bedford Town, lay in wait for the Shrimps at The Eyrie. A late Mal Richmond goal, on the day when football saw its first ever streaker, sent the 1,000 or so Morecambe fans home happy. The two-legged semi against South Shields was, if anything, an anti-climax after the previous ties. The job was done with a 2-0 away victory at Croft Park in the first leg and when Jimmy Sutton scored after seventeen minutes of the second leg to make it 3-0 on aggregate, the crowd of 3,535 could start to think about that wonderful day in late April at the Twin Towers.

Since that day the club have not reached those heights in the competition, though on a number of occasions players, officials and supporters have felt that it would all happen again. A quarter-final appearance in 1976/77, before losing late in the game at Slough, and a third-round defeat to eventual winners Colchester United in 1991/92 were bitter pills to swallow.

However, a 3-2 defeat at Guiseley in 1993/94 was unquestionably the biggest disappointment for Morecambe FC in recent years. The club had over the previous two to three seasons been growing in trophy stature, and so, on reaching the quarter-finals, playing Unibond Division One opposition was seen as difficult but not insurmountable. The disappointment felt by all of Morecambe's fans in the 2,000-plus crowd was total. Beaten as much by themselves as by game but limited opponents, the dream, that appeared to be becoming reality, was swiftly dashed.

Routes to the Final

Morecambe

First round	Mexborough 0, Morecambe 3
Second round	Morecambe 2, Bangor City 1
Third round	Morecambe 0, Kettering Town 0
Third-round replay	Kettering Town 1, Morecambe 2
Fourth round	Bedford Town 0, Morecambe 1
Semi-final, first leg	South Shields 0, Morecambe 2
Semi-final, second leg	Morecambe 1, South Shields 0

Dartford

First round	Ashford Town 2, Dartford 3
Second round	Dartford 0, Minehead 0
Second-round replay	Minehead 1, Dartford 2
Third round	Dartford 1, Banbury United 1
Third-round replay	Banbury United 2, Dartford 2
Third round, second replay (at Bedford)	Dartford 1, Banbury United 0
Fourth round	Weymouth 1, Dartford 2
Semi-final, first leg	Macclesfield Town 1, Dartford 2
Semi-final, second leg	Dartford 0, Macclesfield Town 0

1975

Matlock Town 4, Scarborough 0
Wembley, 26 April 1975

Matlock upset trophy favourites Scarborough with a composed all-round performance that sent the Seasiders reeling with three late goals. The 4-0 scoreline did not tell the full story, as Scarborough spurned several chances to make a game of it while Matlock fully made their opportunities tell. Indeed, it was Boro who started the game more brightly, with Matlock 'keeper David Fell called into action several times in the first quarter of an hour, notably when touching away a shot from Boro's veteran striker Jeff Barmby. But Matlock took the lead on eighteen minutes. Ray Pettit failed to clear and former British Army player Colin Oxley swept the ball into the net as Boro 'keeper Mike Williams advanced.

Scarborough were unruffled, and Pettit nearly atoned with a superb header just past the post with Fell looking beaten. Boro midfielder Ian Davidson also shot wide and on thirty-two minutes Scarborough had a penalty appeal turned down after Matlock player-manager Peter Swan appeared to bring down John Woodall. Scarborough player-boss Ken Houghton saw a goal-bound shot deflected behind for a corner shortly afterwards.

Houghton went close again with a shot just over the bar and winger Tony Aveyard saw an effort blocked. Teenage prodigy Aveyard, in the notebooks of several Football League clubs, caused Matlock problems with his speed and skill, setting up further chances for Barmby and Woodall before half-time.

After the restart, Boro were once again on the offensive, with Woodall, Houghton and Bobby Todd all shooting wide – Woodall's miss being from just five yards – and Sean Marshall's long-range shot well saved by Fell. Aveyard's accurate corners and crosses looked certain to find a hole in Matlock's defence, but the Gladiators stood firm and Boro's relentless surges were beginning to open them up to a Matlock counter-attack.

Above: Matlock station experiences a sudden upsurge in passenger numbers as crowds await a football special to Wembley.

Right: Scarborough goalkeeper Mike Williams keeps his eye on the ball as Dick Hewitt clears.

The sucker punch came on sixty-eight minutes. Mick Fenoughty, one of three Fenoughty brothers in the Matlock side, floated in a high corner that Peter Scott headed on to centre-back Colin Dawson – that day celebrating his twenty-fifth birthday – who hit it home. Six minutes later, Boro were dead and buried. Harry Dunn fouled Mick Fenoughty and his brother Tom sweetly hit the resulting free-kick into the roof of the net from thirty yards or more.

Boro refused to lie down and Houghton, Aveyard and Barmby all tested Fell before Matlock surged forward again in the eighty-second minute. Oxley made a dazzling run to the byline, beating three opponents, and with Scarborough's defence pulled out of shape his cross was headed in by Nick Fenoughty. In the closing seconds Barmby spurned the chance of a consolation when he hooked over with Fell beaten. It summed up Scarborough's day. But Matlock had risen to the occasion. They soaked up pressure, but were ruthless when chances came their way.

'When I saw Tom Fenoughty go up to receive the cup, I thought, "this is Matlock's finest hour",' Swan, who played 19 games for England between 1960 and 1962, said afterwards. 'I was really proud of all our players. The response from everyone at Matlock during the past year – the team, the committee, the supporters – has made me proud too. I have only been at Matlock for one season but I feel that I have been here all my life.' It was an emotional affair, with Wembley's 21,000 spectators rising to Swan, whose career was wrecked by the soccer bribery scandal of the mid-1960s – but this was not compassion. Swan and his opportunist team had thoroughly earned their acclaim.

Meanwhile, Scarborough's attitude in defeat summed up the superb spirit in which the final was played. Ken Houghton was first into the Matlock dressing room to congratulate Swan and Boro's fans applauded Matlock on their lap of honour.

While the Blues basked in glory, it was back to the drawing board for Scarborough. 'We are now going to celebrate our return to Wembley next year,' Scarborough chairman Don Robinson said, without a hint of irony. Prophetic words indeed.

Matlock Town: Fell, McKay, Smith, Stuart, Swan, Dawson, Oxley, N. Fenoughty, Scott, T. Fenoughty, M. Fenoughty. Substitute: Brookes.

Scarborough: Williams, Hewitt, Pettit, Dunn, Marshall, Todd, Houghton, Woodall, Davidson, Barmby, Aveyard. Substitute: Fountain.

In Focus
Matlock's Greatest Day

Matlock Town's stunning 1975 FA Trophy triumph put the club firmly on the non-League map and remains to this day their finest hour. Their Wembley success was part of a purple patch under the player-management of former England international defender Peter Swan, who took over at the club during the summer of 1974. Swan's impact was swift and in December 1974 Matlock showed what they were capable of by winning 10-0 at Lancaster City, a record Northern Premier League victory that was to stand until 2000.

Safely placed in mid-table in the Northern Premier League – a big improvement on the previous two seasons – Matlock were able to concentrate on the cups, reaching the first round of the FA Cup, where they lost 4-1 at home to Division Three Champions Blackburn Rovers.

Matlock also beat Glossop to win the Derbyshire Senior Cup for the first time, but it was the FA Trophy that provided the enduring memories. Starting in the third qualifying round, they played nine matches to make it to Wembley, coming through replays against Burscough in the second round and Ilford in the third. The Twin Towers seemed to be slipping from view when Matlock lost the home leg of their semi-final against Burton Albion 1-0, in front of a record 5,123 crowd. But goals from Peter Scott and Nick Fenoughty sealed a 2-0 win at Burton to win 2-1 on aggregate.

On the crest of a wave after beating Scarborough, Swan steered Matlock into fourth place in the Northern Premier League in 1975/76, but left the club the following summer. Tom Fenoughty took over the reins and once again put Matlock in the limelight, taking them to the FA Cup third round for the only time in their history after an amazing 5-2 win at Division Three Champions-elect Mansfield Town in the second round.

Strong performances continued in the Northern Premier League – they missed out on the championship by just 2 points in 1976/77 – but, despite a third-place finish in 1978/79, Matlock did not join the newly formed Alliance Premier League.

This marked the end of Matlock's golden period. Tom Fenoughty resigned in November 1980 and a brief return by Peter Swan failed to revive former glories. Mick Fenoughty replaced him and under his management Matlock finished second in the Northern Premier League in 1983/84, a height they have failed to emulate since. In 1995/96 Matlock were relegated from the UniBond Premier League and have remained in Division One.

Matlock have never applied to join the Football League, and with current crowds hovering around the 300 mark, the Nationwide Conference would probably be a bridge too far. However, a return to the Premier Division of the UniBond League or the soon-to-be-formed Conference Division Two would certainly not be beyond their ambitions.

Routes to the Final

Matlock Town

Third qualifying round	Tamworth 0, Matlock Town 1
First round	Matlock Town 3, Kings Lynn 0
Second round	Burscough 1, Matlock Town 1
Second-round replay	Matlock Town 3, Burscough 1
Third round	Matlock Town 1, Ilford 1
Third-round replay	Ilford 0, Matlock Town 1
Fourth round	Goole Town 0, Matlock Town 1
Semi-final, first leg	Matlock Town 0, Burton Albion 1
Semi-final, second leg	Burton Albion 0, Matlock Town 2

Scarborough

First round	Scarborough 4, Gateshead 0
Second round	Boston United 1, Scarborough 1
Second-round replay	Scarborough 1, Boston United 0
Third round	Scarborough 2, Enfield 1
Fourth round	Scarborough 1, Wimbledon 0
Semi-final, first leg	Scarborough 3, Bedford Town 1
Semi-final, second leg	Bedford Town 1, Scarborough 3

1976

Scarborough 3, Stafford Rangers 2
Wembley, 24 April 1976

Previous trophy winners Scarborough and Stafford Rangers served up a pulsating final that needed extra time to separate the two sides. It was a match that oozed drama from start to finish and truly did not deserve to have a loser. In the end, Scarborough fulfilled their vow to bury the memories of their loss in the final the previous year.

Stafford set the tone of the match by taking the lead after just five minutes. Barry Lowe saw his shot blocked. It fell to Stuart Chapman, who fired against the bar, before striker Roger Jones scored his first FA Trophy goal of the season with a shot that deflected past Scarborough 'keeper Geoff Barnard.

Scarborough quickly picked themselves up, with Harry Dunn shooting just wide and Stafford 'keeper Jim Arnold cutting out several dangerous crosses. But Stafford responded with headers from Roger Jones and Bob Ritchie, both narrowly off target.

Boro stalwart Chris Dale, a late surprise call-up to the side, responded by playing out of his skin on the right side and causing all sorts of problems for Stafford. Firstly a cross from Dale was headed to safety, and soon afterwards Arnold had to race out of his goal to prevent a Dale centre reaching star striker John Woodall.

It was Woodall who levelled the scores just before half-time. The Stafford defence failed to properly clear a Harry A. Dunn corner and Woodall fired accurately through a crowd of players.

Stafford regained the lead just two minutes after the interval. Jim Sargeant, in his tenth season at Stafford, flighted over a free-kick, and Roger Jones, always dangerous in the air, headed home. Barely had Stafford finished their celebrations when Dale produced an almost carbon-copy free-kick at the other end, but Billy Ayre's header was tipped onto the post by Arnold.

Boro equalised on fifty-four minutes, when a Harry A. Dunn corner was knocked on by Ayre for Derek Abbey to score with an unstoppable header. Jeff Barmby then had a shot blocked and hit another wide before limping off with a leg injury, to be substituted by Gerry Donoghue on sixty-three minutes.

Stafford also brought on their substitute John Ritchie and he nearly wrapped things up for Rangers with a header that Barnard saved brilliantly before foiling Colin Chadwick's follow-up. Both sides continued to push for a winner right up to the final whistle, with Abbey just failing to reach a Dale centre before Dale himself produced an overhead kick that landed on the roof of the net.

Boro began to edge proceedings in extra time and on 101 minutes were awarded a penalty when Stafford centre-back Ben Seddon brought down Dave Hilley.

Above: The Stafford Rangers squad that reached Wembley in 1976. From left to right, back row: John Overath (trainer), Barry Whittaker (physio), Hugh McLeish, John Ritchie, Ben Seddon, Mick Morris, Colin Chadwick, Jim Arnold, Bob Fletcher, Colin Meldrum (manager), Bob Ritchie (captain), Archie Richards. Front row: Jim Sargeant, Stuart Hutchison, Stuart Chapman, Roger Jones, Dave Seddon, Barry Lowe, Tony Keyes, Kevin Hughes.

Left: Scarborough's Chris Dale responded to a surprise call-up by playing a key role in the 1976 final.

Woodall hit his spot kick firmly but Stafford's Man of the Match Arnold dived the right way to pull off an amazing save. In the second period of extra time, Arnold once again defied Woodall, turning away a powerful twenty-yard shot.

With just two minutes remaining, the sides looked set for a replay at Bramall Lane only for the game to take its final dramatic turn. Seddon was again judged to be the sinner for Stafford with a handball in the area and this time Boro defender Sean Marshall stepped up confidently and sent Arnold the wrong way with a well-placed penalty. After a game that must rank among Wembley's best, Scarborough chairman John Fawcett reflected it seemed tragic that somebody had to lose. But Boro won, thanks to a never-say-die spirit and the endless effort they put in. Stafford, who matched Boro all the way, were left to console themselves – but with a vow to return soon.

Scarborough: Barnard, Jackson, Marshall, Dunn, Ayre, Harry A. Dunn, Dale, Barmby, Abbey, Woodall, Hilley. Substitute: Donoghue.

Stafford Rangers: Arnold, B. Ritchie, Richards, Sargeant, B. Seddon, Morris, Chapman, Lowe, Jones, Hutchison, Chadwick. Substitute: J. Ritchie.

In Focus
My First Time

(BBC Sport Online's football editor, Howard Nurse, recalls his first trip to Wembley in 1976)

Do you know the feeling when your team wins a cup semi-final and it dawns on you that your club is going to be playing at Wembley?

It is one of the best feelings; the sheer excitement of the thought of going to Wembley is almost indescribable. For me, this happened when I was just ten years old. It was the most exhilarating day of my first decade. I had only become seriously interested in football the previous summer and now I was lucky enough to have the chance to see my home-town club play beneath the famous Twin Towers of Wembley.

Almost twenty-five years on, and I can remember as vividly as though it was only yesterday how we set off on a rickety old British Rail train early that Saturday morning. Not only was it my very first trip to the home of football, but it was also my first adventure to London. From Scarborough, it seemed like a million miles away (it was only 240). King's Cross to Wembley was my first experience of the London Underground and our excitement was almost uncontrollable as we first set eyes on the Twin Towers.

Up Wembley Way we walked. The anticipation was building. We were about to go inside the world's most famous stadium. Fans from both teams mingled in the friendliest of atmospheres before kick-off, but all I wanted to do was get my first glimpse inside the ground. The fans streamed in and the atmosphere soon became electric. Everyone seemed to be wearing scarves and rosettes and were waving huge banners and shouting at the tops of their voices.

The teams came out to rapturous applause. Next was the national anthem and we were ready to start. Expectations were sky-high in both camps. Sadly, one team had to lose. The drama was about to unfold.

It was nerve wracking and the game seemed to fly by so quickly. Scarborough did not start particularly well and we trailed 2-1 deep into the second half. But we refused to lie down and die. We had lost at Wembley 4-0 in the final the previous season and were not about to repeat that. The equaliser came late in normal time and an extra thirty minutes of extra time were required. That was great, I thought, because nobody was in a rush to leave the famous stadium.

The action switched from end-to-end as both sides bravely sought a winner. There were near misses for both teams, but when the final went into injury time of extra time, a replay at Bramall Lane looked a certainty.

'Handball!'

One last push. 'Handball, referee' – it must be a penalty. It was – and what's more, it was going to be the last kick of the game. Up stepped Sean Marshall and the ball flew past goalkeeper John Arnold, smashing against the back of the net to spark scenes of hysteria in our section of the crowd. The glittering silver trophy was proudly lifted high into the air by captain Harry Dunn. We had won the 1976 FA Trophy, beating Stafford Rangers 3-2 after extra time.

The celebrations went on in the car park outside and what seemed like the whole population of our town started the journey back north. How that journey seemed so much shorter with a Wembley win under our belts! There's no place like Wembley – especially when you're just a kid.

Routes to the Final

Scarborough

First round	Scarborough 3, Willington 2
Second round	Goole Town 1, Scarborough 1
Second-round replay	Scarborough 3, Goole Town 1
Third round	Scarborough 3, Dagenham 0
Fourth round	Scarborough 1, Tooting & Mitcham United 0
Semi-final, first leg	Scarborough 1, Enfield 0
Semi-final, second leg	Enfield 0, Scarborough 0

Stafford Rangers

First round	Stafford Rangers 4, Burscough 0
Second round	Burton Albion 0, Stafford Rangers 1
Third round	Stafford Rangers 2, Matlock Town 1
Fourth round	Stafford Rangers 2, Hillingdon Borough 0
Semi-final, first leg	Stafford Rangers 1, Runcorn 0
Semi-final, second leg	Runcorn 0, Stafford Rangers 0

1977

Scarborough 2, Dagenham 1
Wembley, 14 May 1977

Scarborough retained the FA Trophy with a dramatic late comeback to stun Dagenham, with Boro's veteran striker Jeff Barmby being the catalyst. On the back foot for long periods of the game and 1-0 down with just six minutes remaining, Boro levelled the scores and then snatched a last-gasp winner when extra time looked on the cards.

The game turned on its head in the eighty-fifth minute. Boro substitute Jeff Barmby, making his fourth Scarborough Wembley appearance, made a penetrating run down the right and crossed to Derek Abbey. Abbey's shot was handled on the line by Dagenham's teenage defender Peter Wellman and Harry A. Dunn made no mistake with his spot kick.

Barmby, in the twilight of his Boro career that began back in 1969/70, continued to cause all sorts of problems for Dagenham, with another surging run winning a corner. Then, with just one minute left on the clock, Barmby again brought the ball forward down the right and squared it to Abbey, who simply guided the ball into the corner of the net.

For Boro's 8,000 travelling fans, including five trainloads, the long journey back to North Yorkshire was suddenly one to savour – an outcome that had looked most unlikely after Dagenham had taken the lead in the twenty-third minute. After a bright opening start, Dagenham's goal was no more than they deserved. Top scorer Mal Harkins' penetrating cross was met by a diving header from Terry Harris that gave Boro 'keeper Dave Chapman no chance. Dagenham continued to hold the upper hand and came close to extending their lead when Chapman did well to smother the ball in a packed goalmouth after Neville Fox sent over a dangerous cross. After the interval it was much the same story and on fifty-three minutes the Daggers had a goal disallowed. Harkins was the provider for long-serving

Dagenham midfielder Jimmy Holder to shoot past Chapman, only for the whistle to blow for offside.

That setback seemed to spur Boro on and they began to look more threatening with a series of corners. However, it was the entry of Barmby as a substitute for the injured Sean Marshall on sixty-three minutes that triggered Boro's rousing finale.

Scarborough manager Colin Appleton said, 'We were confident in the dressing room at half-time that things would go right for us. If our equaliser had come earlier, we would not have had that frantic last few minutes.' In addition, Appleton believed that Boro's string of FA Trophy wins could help propel them into the Football League. 'Boro's big support and record in the competition speaks volumes for Scarborough people, its football and its potential as a Division Four club', he declared.

Scarborough were to get a bite of the Football League cherry – but they had to wait another ten years to enter Division Four as the first club to gain automatic promotion to the League. However, their Wembley successes greatly raised the profile of the club and sowed the seeds for the progress into the Alliance Premier League and on to the Football League.

Sadly, the final became one surrounded by two personal tragedies. The father-in-law of Dagenham manager Laurie Wilkinson collapsed and died soon after Dagenham scored. Then, three days after the final, Scarborough player Tony Aveyard died as a result of head injuries following a clash of heads in a Northern Premier League match against Boston United. Twenty-one-year-old Aveyard was a gifted winger who had trials with Manchester City, Arsenal and Burnley and his death stunned the town. The Boro players immediately gave their Wembley earnings and bonuses to an appeal fund for Aveyard's widow. Over 3,000 spectators turned out to pay tribute to Aveyard in a Northern Premier League game against Northwich Victoria, played the day after his death.

Dagenham: Huttley, Wellman, P. Currie, Dunwell, Moore, W. Currie, Harkins, Saul, Fox, Harris, Holder. Substitute: Scales.

Scarborough: Chapman, Smith, Marshall, Dunn, Ayre, Deere, Aveyard, Donoghue, Woodall, Abbey, Harry A. Dunn. Substitute: Barmby.

In Focus
Boro's Marathon Trophy Route

Scarborough only reached Wembley after an extraordinary quest involving 12 games and a semi-final tussle with Altrincham that involved four matches and lasted 420 minutes. Boro needed replays to beat Walthamstow Avenue, Hitchin Town, Nuneaton Borough and Altrincham (twice), with the initial game against Nuneaton abandoned at half-time! The resultant huge fixture pile-up extended Boro's season into late May.

Above: Scarborough goalkeeper David Chapman cannot bear to look as Harry A. Dunn takes Boro's equalising penalty.

Right: Derek Abbey was on hand to force home Scarborough's late winner.

DAGENHAM F.C.
F.A. Trophy Final

SOUVENIR
1976-77

25p

The magnificence of Wembley Stadium from the air was illustrated on this official Dagenham souvenir brochure of the 1977 final.

It all began with a first-round tie at home to Frickley that only just passed a pitch inspection after heavy rain. With snow falling during the match, Boro adapted best in the mud-bath conditions and goals from Harry Dunn and Derek Abbey saw them through.

There was little respite in the second round as Boro travelled to dual Amateur Cup winners Walthamstow Avenue. If anything, the pitch in London E17 was even worse; a muddy morass sanded heavily down the middle. Scarborough settled for a 0-0 draw and four days later, in – you guessed it – heavy rain, Boro beat Walthamstow 2-1, coming from behind with goals from John Woodall and Jeff Barmby.

True to form, underfoot conditions were sticky for the third-round tie at Hitchin Town. Boro came away with a 0-0 draw, but spurned several opportunities to win and it was no surprise that they triumphed in the replay at the Athletic Ground. Tony Aveyard turned on the style to steer Boro through. He provided the cross for Chris Dale to score after just three minutes and then set up John Woodall in similar fashion just after the interval. Woodall put the game beyond doubt with a stunning long-range shot just seconds after the restart.

The weather again menaced Scarborough in the fourth round, forcing the abandonment of their home game against Nuneaton Borough, with the Seasiders 2-0 up. Heavy rain fell on an already sodden pitch and, despite efforts by supporters and staff to mop up at half-time, the game was called off during the interval. When the match was restarted just four days later, more than 100 fans used forks beforehand to help remove surface water. Boro looked likely to win when John Woodall opened up the Nuneaton defence and scored, but an equaliser before half-time shocked the Seasiders. Scarborough dominated the second half but could not find a way through and had to travel to Nuneaton on Monday 28 March – the sides' third meeting in eleven days. Over 500 Boro fans made the trip and were rewarded with victory, thanks to a goal that glanced in off Jeff Barmby as Scarborough withstood considerable Nuneaton pressure.

Scarborough finally had good, sunny conditions for their semi-final first leg at home to Altrincham on 9 April, and with goals from Billy Ayre and Harry A. Dunn, Boro looked on their way to Wembley, but six days later Altrincham turned on the style at Moss Lane and two second-half strikes levelled the aggregate scores. Scarborough had the upper hand in extra time after Altrincham's Joe Flaherty was sent off, but could not find a goal, with Jeff Barmby hitting the bar. On Wednesday 20 April the sides met for the replay at Rotherham, where Altrincham were awarded a penalty only for Mick Moore to hit the post with his spot kick and the game ended 0-0 after extra time. But the following Monday, Scarborough finally completed their gruelling road to Wembley. A second replay at Doncaster, in front of 3,761 spectators, saw a Billy Ayre header and yet another fine finish from John Woodall secure a 2-1 win, with the players mobbed by jubilant spectators at the final whistle.

Routes to the Final

Scarborough

First round	Scarborough 3, Frickley Athletic 1
Second round	Walthamstow Avenue 0, Scarborough 0
Second-round replay	Scarborough 2, Walthamstow Avenue 1
Third round	Hitchin Town 0, Scarborough 0
Third-round replay	Scarborough 3, Hitchin Town 1
Fourth round	Scarborough 2, Nuneaton Borough 0 (abandoned after forty-five minutes)
Fourth round	Scarborough 1, Nuneaton Borough 1
Fourth-round replay	Nuneaton Borough 0, Scarborough 1
Semi-final, first leg	Scarborough 2, Altrincham 0
Semi-final, second leg	Altrincham 2, Scarborough 0
Semi-final replay) (at Rotherham)	Scarborough 0, Altrincham 0
Semi-final, second replay (at Doncaster)	Scarborough 2, Altrincham 1

Dagenham

First round	Leatherhead 1, Dagenham 1
First-round replay	Dagenham 2, Leatherhead 0
Second round	Dagenham 1, Yeovil Town 1
Second-round replay	Yeovil Town 1, Dagenham 2
Third round	Dagenham 1, Runcorn 0
Fourth round	Chorley 1, Dagenham 1
Fourth-round replay	Dagenham 5, Chorley 1
Semi-final, first leg	Dagenham 3, Slough Town 0
Semi-final, second leg	Slough Town 2, Dagenham 3

1978

Altrincham 3, Leatherhead 1
Wembley, 29 April 1978

Altrincham captured the FA Trophy in a game in which they could do no wrong. It was a game of high excitement, in which Leatherhead played a worthy part, but the trophy was heading north from the first few minutes. Altrincham looked the slicker and more confident of the two sides and stamped their authority in just the second minute. Leading goalscorer Jeff Johnson, who had a spell with Stockport County during the season, burst down the left and delivered a piercing cross that was met on the volley by John Rogers. Altrincham were one up from their first attack.

From then on, the Robins never looked back. Johnson and Rogers tore the Leatherhead defence apart, ably assisted by winger Ian Morris. John Davison took a grip in the middle of the park, with captain John King and Graham Heathcote completing a formidable trio in midfield.

But Leatherhead were not without their stars. The feared striking duo of Chris Kelly and John Baker, whose goals had helped propel Leatherhead to Wembley, showed some clever touches, but the Tanners found the going tough at the back. They were frequently in trouble, especially down the left flank, where John Cooper showed great style on the attack but struggled to combine this with handling Altrincham's relentless raids.

Leatherhead's defence looked leaky after Altrincham's opener and on fourteen minutes the Robins were two up. Leatherhead failed to clear and Johnson slammed the ball past 'keeper John Swannell. Nevertheless, the Tanners were unlucky not to go in at half-time with a shout. On thirty-nine minutes John Baker set up Kelly, who unleashed a powerful drive that hit the bar. But the Robins could point to the greater number of chances and towards the interval whistle Stan Allan and Johnson both went close.

Soon after the restart it was all over. King rose to head the third and there was no way back for Leatherhead. To their eternal credit, the Tanners' heads did not drop where lesser sides could have folded. They continued to battle and Altrincham goal-keeper Peter Eales was alert to save from Cooper midway in the half. It was just reward when on eighty-four minutes Micky Cook was on hand to gain a consolation goal.

But Altrincham remained on the boil and Davison and substitute Joe Flaherty both went close as the Robins confidently retained control of the vital areas of the Wembley turf. The Robins had taken the home of football by storm in one of their best ever performances. Altrincham's players ran to their 12,000 fans at the end of the game and the supporters passed scarves, banners and flags over to their heroes. Coach Peter Warburton said, 'It was an amazing feeling in the dressing room afterwards. Graham Heys, who was in the squad but did not play, was crying his eyes out for joy.'

Altrincham: Eales, Allan, Crossley, Bailey, Owens, King, Morris, Heathcote, Johnson, Rogers, Davison. Substitute: Flaherty.

Leatherhead: Swannell, Cooper, Eaton, Davies, Reid, Malley, Cook, Salkeld, Kelly, Baker, Doyle. Substitute: Bailey.

In Focus
The Seventies were Glory Years for Leatherhead

(With thanks to Leatherhead FC)

Leatherhead's FA Trophy final appearance came in the midst of a period of unprecedented success for Leatherhead that has not even been approached since. The club, as it is currently known, came into being in May 1946, when two local Leatherhead clubs, Leatherhead Rose and Leatherhead United, merged, and as Leatherhead Football Club they entered the Surrey Senior League.

The Tanners, as they were nicknamed, won four successive championships, before transferring to the Metropolitan League for one season. In 1951, Leatherhead became founder members of the Delphian League, before progressing, in 1958, to the Corinthian League. 1963 was the final season of that league, and Leatherhead finished the season as its champions. The Corinthian League then merged with the Athenian League, and in 1964 Leatherhead won Division One, thus earning promotion to the Premier Division.

In 1969, Leatherhead won its only Surrey Senior Cup success, defeating Redhill 3-1 at Sutton United's Gander Green Lane ground. Leatherhead also added the Surrey Senior Shield and the Surrey Intermediate Cup that year. This was the first occasion in which one club achieved this feat, and the Surrey FA awarded Leatherhead a special plaque to commemorate this still unique achievement.

The seventies were nothing short of spectacular for the Tanners. In 1971, Leatherhead reached the first of their two FA Amateur Cup semi-finals, losing 2-0 at Bolton's Burnden Park ground to the eventual winners Skelmersdale United. Two seasons later, the Tanners won election to the Isthmian League, and a year after that, in 1974, Leatherhead again reached the FA Amateur Cup semi-final. This time they were beaten 1–0 at Millwall's Den by Ilford. Ilford were then beaten 4–1 in the final by Bishop's Stortford, in what became the last FA Amateur Cup final. The 1974/75 season saw Leatherhead reach the FA Cup first round proper for the first time, and in so doing they hit the headlines with a bang.

Bishop's Stortford were beaten in a replay in the first round, before the Tanners dispatched Colchester United in the second round. Then, incredibly, Brighton and Hove Albion were beaten by the odd goal at the Goldstone Ground in the third round. After that came Leicester City, at home in the fourth round, a match which was switched to Filbert Street. Around 32,000 people saw a dramatic match in which Peter McGillicuddy and Chris Kelly put the Tanners two goals up, and then saw a potential third cleared off the line before Leicester City fought back to win 3–2. Further FA Cup victories against a Ron Atkinson-managed Cambridge United in 1975 and Northampton Town in 1976 cemented Leatherhead's reputation as a giant-killer.

Leatherhead finally reached Wembley in 1978 for the FA Trophy final, but were soundly beaten 3–1 by an excellent Altrincham side. That season saw Leatherhead also become losing finalists in the Isthmian League Cup and reach the first round of the FA Cup for a fourth time, where they were beaten by Swansea City. The second round was reached in 1979, with Colchester United gaining revenge for their defeat in 1974/75. They reached the first round for the last time to date in 1980/81.

Unfortunately, in 1983, the Tanners endured a wretched season, being relegated from the Premier Division. On the way, eventual champions Sutton United defeated

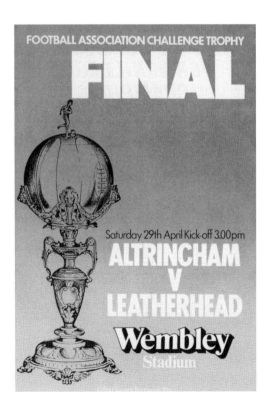

Match programme from the 1978 Altrincham
v. Leatherhead Wembley FA Trophy final.

them 11-1. Two seasons later, Leatherhead were denied promotion on goal difference by Kingstonian. During that season, the Tanners had 3 points deducted for an ineligible player.

The 1980s as a whole proved to be a struggle, as a succession of managers worked tirelessly in the name of Leatherhead. Billy Miller, Martin Hinshelwood (formerly of Crystal Palace), Keith Mills, Micky Cook, Micky Leach (former QPR player), Roger Charland, Keith Oram, Adam Hill, John Cassidy, Mickey Byrne and Terry Eames all worked hard to achieve some sort of success as well as avoiding relegation. The only major highlights were a defeat inflicted upon Wycombe Wanderers in the FA Trophy and a Southern Combination Cup final win in 1990, beating Malden Vale to win the cup. Unfortunately, that same season saw the Tanners relegated to Division Two. In June 1995 the club converted to a limited company, and the new board of directors set about improving matters, with significant ground improvements being undertaken.

In 1996/97, under Keith Wenham's management, Leatherhead scored 116 goals, finished runners-up to Collier Row & Romford, and achieved promotion to the Ryman League Division One. Sadly, several seasons of struggle followed, with the club being relegated back to Division Two in 2000/01. With ongoing league reorganisation, Leatherhead moved into Division One (South) for the 2002/03 season.

Routes to the Final

Altrincham

First round	Workington 0, Altrincham 0
First-round replay	Altrincham 4, Workington 0
Second round	Altrincham 4, Frickley Athletic 0
Third round	Matlock Town 1, Altrincham 1
Third-round replay	Altrincham 2, Matlock Town 0
Fourth round	Altrincham 4, Winsford United 2
Semi-final, first leg	Altrincham 0, Runcorn 0
Semi-final, second leg	Runcorn 0, Altrincham 1

Leatherhead

First round	Banbury United 1, Leatherhead 2
Second round	Leatherhead 5, Dartford 1
Third round	Leatherhead 2, Wigan Athletic 0
Fourth round	Bedford Town 0, Leatherhead 0
Fourth-round replay	Leatherhead 5, Bedford Town 2
Semi-final, first leg	Leatherhead 2, Spennymoor United 0
Semi-final, second leg	Spennymoor United 2, Leatherhead 1

1979

Stafford Rangers 2, Kettering Town 0
Wembley, 19 May 1979

Stafford manager Roy Chapman masterminded Rangers' second FA Trophy success in seven years as two Alf Wood goals brought the prize back to Marston Road. Stafford's players followed Chapman's instructions to the letter to contain the Poppies, and then hit them ruthlessly on the breaks. 'We knew how we would approach the game and how Kettering would play,' explained Chapman. 'The players carried out my instructions to the last word and that was one of the most pleasing things about the victory.'

In front of a record-breaking 32,000 crowd, Rangers were the side most under pressure, but Wood executed with deadly accuracy two of the four scoring chances that his side had. In addition, Chapman appointed twenty-year-old Wayne Secker to mark Kettering goal machine Billy Kellock and the Southern League's top scorer rarely got a look in. Central defenders Ben Seddon and Bob Ritchie, who kept tabs on Kettering's other forwards Peter Phipps and Roy Clayton, ably aided Secker.

Stafford's long-serving midfielder Jim Sargeant, who appeared for Stafford in both previous finals, said, 'Roy gave us a good insight on Kettering. We stifled them when it really mattered.' Stafford's back line held firm in the opening thirty minutes when Kettering called the shots and even Wood was called upon to help out in defence. But the Poppies were mainly limited to long-range attempts. The closest that they came to scoring was on the half hour when Phipps cut in and had a drive bravely kept out by Stafford 'keeper Jim Arnold. The ball fell again to Phipps, who crossed to the unmarked Fred Easthall. His shot was true but Seddon somehow headed the ball away to safety.

The first of Wood's two goals followed just four minutes later. Following a build-up by Stuart Chapman and Mick Cullerton, Wood managed to slip between two defenders and swept the ball home with his right foot.

Left: Captain Bob Ritchie lifts the FA Trophy aloft after Stafford Rangers had beaten Kettering Town 2-0 at Wembley.

Opposite: Mick Cullerton's goal in the semi-final second leg sent Stafford on their way to Wembley with a 1-1 draw at home to Runcorn, Rangers having won the first leg 2-1.

The killer blow came on sixty-five minutes. Once again, Cullerton and Chapman were the architects, the latter setting up Cullerton, whose shot was blocked before falling to Wood, who made no mistake. Late in the game, with Rangers almost home and dry, Arnold was alert to make a point-blank save from Phipps and ensure a nerveless last few minutes for Stafford.

Stafford captain Bob Ritchie – a Kettering-born player – said, 'This was one of my proudest moments and certainly made up for the defeat against Scarborough.' Top scorer Cullerton, in his second spell with Rangers, added: 'I feel better than in 1972, because against Barnet we were expected to win. This time, everybody expected a close game and we came through well. Once ahead, I could not see us losing.'

It was third-time lucky for winger Colin Chadwick, who in 1973 missed the chance to play in the final with Wigan Athletic and was a member of Rangers' losing side in 1976. 'It's a great feeling that hasn't really sunk in,' he said after the match. 'But I always felt, after we scored, that we would win.'

Stafford Rangers: Arnold, F. Wood, Willis, Sargeant, Seddon, Ritchie, Secker, Chapman, A. Wood, Cullerton, Chadwick. Substitute: Jones.

Kettering Town: Lane, Ashby, Lee, Easthall, Dixey, Suddards, Flannagan, Kellock, Phipps, Clayton, Evans. Substitute: Hughes.

In Focus
Kettering Town: Non-League's Nearly Men

While 19 May 1979 belonged to Stafford Rangers, Kettering's presence was yet another illustration of their claims to League status – claims that have never borne fruit despite over a century of trying. Indeed, Kettering's long-suffering supporters can afford a moment of bitter reflection that their club has never had much greater success: two FA Trophy finals – both on the losing side – eighteen applications to join the Football League and four Nationwide Conference runners-up spots – the latest, in 1998/99, just 4 points behind champions Cheltenham.

The long-term reward for such consistency is that Kettering currently reside far away from the non-League limelight with mid-table anonymity in the Ryman League, but memories such as those of the 1978/79 season serve to remind that it was not always thus.

The 1970s were arguably Kettering's golden age. While the club made several previous Football League applications, including six on the trot between 1957 and 1962, they had never really been considered major contenders. This changed in 1973, when, having won the Southern League Championship under the management of Ron Atkinson, Kettering gained twelve votes in their bid for League election.

Between 1974 and 1976, Kettering were snapping at the Football League's heels, gaining sixteen votes to Workington's twenty-one in 1974 and again being held at bay by the Cumbrians in 1975 with twenty votes to twenty-eight for the League members. Ironically, when Workington's luck finally ran out in 1977, a new ruling restricting the number of applicants to two meant that it was Wimbledon who entered the League's door.

October 1977 saw Mick Jones succeed Derek Dougan as manager at Rockingham Road. Jones, a former Derby County favourite in one of the club's most successful periods under Brian Clough, came to Kettering after injury ended his playing career prematurely. Jones, beginning a long managerial career that at the time of writing sees him in charge at Telford United, instilled an iron discipline among his squad that saw any dissent or retaliation on the field costing them a week's wages. His methods worked, with 1978/79 seeing not only the Wembley appearance but also a runners-up spot in the Southern League, with 109 goals scored, thanks to the prolific scoring trio of Roy Clayton, Peter Phipps and captain Billy Kellock.

At Wembley, many of the supporters understandably thought that Kettering did not do themselves justice after such a free-scoring season, but still lined the route to Rockingham Road to welcome Jones and his team back home.

Routes to the Final

Kettering Town

First round	Kettering Town 1, Nuneaton Borough 1
First-round replay	Nuneaton Borough 0, Kettering Town 1
Second round	Kettering Town 3, Scarborough 0
Third round	Kettering Town 2, Maidstone United 0
Fourth round	Kettering Town 1, Enfield 1
Fourth-round replay	Enfield 0, Kettering Town 3
Semi-final, first leg	Dagenham 0, Kettering Town 0
Semi-final, second leg	Kettering Town 1, Dagenham 0

Stafford Rangers

First round	Stafford Rangers 1, Matlock Town 1
First-round replay	Matlock Town 1, Stafford Rangers 2
Second round	Weymouth 0, Stafford Rangers 1
Third round	Stafford Rangers 2, Boston United 1
Fourth round	Bishop Auckland 1, Stafford Rangers 1
Fourth-round replay	Stafford Rangers 3, Bishop Auckland 1
Semi-final, first leg	Runcorn 1, Stafford Rangers 2
Semi-final, second leg	Stafford Rangers 1, Runcorn 1

1980

Dagenham 2, Mossley 1
Wembley, 17 May 1980

Dagenham put aside three previous Wembley disappointments in the 1970s to narrowly overcome Mossley. The Daggers had suffered two FA Amateur Trophy defeats, followed by a last-gasp loss to Scarborough in the 1977 FA Trophy final. This time they just edged out a gritty Mossley side to take the trophy south for the first time in its history.

Mossley came to their first Wembley visit as Northern Premier League Champions and had 32 successive games without defeat behind them. It was not difficult to understand why. They had a superb goalkeeper in John Fitton and captain Leo Skeete covered every inch of the park in defence. Colleagues who gave no quarter backed them.

But Dagenham had great composure, notably at the back, where Peter Wellman, Denis Moore, Tommy Horan and Terry Scales were magnificent. When that line was breached, goalkeeper Ian Huttley was in fine form. Joe Durrell, brought into midfield for the injured Jimmy Holder, played as if he was the regular choice and Joe Dunwell and Steve Jones served the nippy front line of Chris Maycock, George Duck and Ricky Kidd plenty of opportunities.

Indeed, it was Dagenham who were fastest out of the blocks. Former Rochdale and Oldham 'keeper Fitton twice foiled Dagenham in the first fourteen minutes, notably with a tremendous save to turn a Kidd shot around the post. But it was a warning of things to come and Fitton was beaten on fifteen minutes when Duck looped in a header from a Durrell centre. Mossley were stung into action and Skeete began to lead by example, first heading just wide and then seeing a shot cleared off the line by Scales. Shortly afterwards, the grounded Huttley still managed to block a shot from Dave Vaughan.

Dagenham should have increased their lead seven minutes before half-time, when Maycock missed contact close in from a Duck centre. Then Fitton kept Mossley hanging on by parrying a close-range shot from Kidd and then getting his hand to a follow-up header. Mossley brought record signing Phil Wilson on for David Moore after the interval and the former Altrincham player quickly made his mark. On forty-nine minutes he put in a cross from the right to the far post, where it was headed back for prolific scorer Ian Smith to hook the ball high into the roof of the net.

Thoughts of another Wembley defeat could have crept in for the Daggers but they steadied themselves and a flurry of three corners put their supporters in good voice. With eight minutes left on the clock, Maycock made up for his earlier missed chance with a brilliant individual goal to cap the tie. Having beaten two defenders, the former Tottenham youth player beat one of them again for good measure and then hit a perfect angled shot past the onrushing Fitton. Maycock had the ball in the net again three minutes from time, but Duck was offside. In the last moments, Scales diverted a Wilson shot for a corner and the trophy was Dagenham's.

Delighted Dagenham manager Eddie Presland praised both sides for a close match played in the right spirit. Presland, who played football for West Ham and first-class cricket for Essex before moving into management, said, 'It was a great advertisement for non-League football. We had the first half, they took the second, but if we had lost it would have been due to their 'keeper. Against a lesser player than Fitton we would have been three up at half-time. We paced ourselves well and it stood us in good stead when we came under pressure in the second half.'

Dagenham: Huttley, Wellman, Scales, Dunwell, Moore, Maycock, Durrell, Horan, Duck, Kidd, Jones. Substitute: Holder.

Mossley: Fitton, Brown, Vaughan, Gorman, Salter, Pollitt, Smith, Moore, Skeete, O'Connor, Keelan. Substitute: Wilson.

In Focus
Daggers Deserved Success

Dagenham finally got their hands on the FA Trophy in 1980 after a series of consistent performances in the competition since first entering it in 1974/75 – and after twice reaching FA Amateur Cup finals at Wembley in the 1970s. Despite starting in the trophy's qualifying stages in 1974/75 and 1975/76, Dagenham never failed to get to at least the third round in every season up to and including 1979/80.

1974/75

Preliminary round	Tilbury 1, Dagenham 1
Preliminary-round replay	Dagenham 2, Tilbury 2
Preliminary round, second replay	Tilbury 2, Dagenham 4
First qualifying round	Dagenham 3, Hayes 0
Second qualifying round	Bognor Regis Town 0, Dagenham 3
Third qualifying round	Dagenham 3, Slough Town 0
First round	Witney Town 2, Dagenham 2
First-round replay	Dagenham 3, Witney Town 0

Second round	Dagenham 1, Canterbury City 1
Second-round replay	Canterbury City 0, Dagenham 2
Third round	Dagenham 1, Weymouth 0
Fourth round	Dagenham 1, Burton Albion 3

1975/76

Third qualifying round	Barking 1, Dagenham 1
Third qualifying-round replay	Dagenham 5, Barking 0
First round	Dartford 1, Dagenham 3
Second round	Wimbledon 0, Dagenham 0
Second-round replay	Dagenham 2, Wimbledon 0
Third round	Scarborough 3, Dagenham 0

1976/77

First round	Leatherhead 1, Dagenham 1
First-round replay	Dagenham 2, Leatherhead 0
Second round	Dagenham 1, Yeovil Town 1
Second-round replay	Yeovil Town 1, Dagenham 2
Third round	Dagenham 1, Runcorn 0
Fourth round	Chorley 1, Dagenham 1
Fourth-round replay	Dagenham 5, Chorley 1
Semi-final, first leg	Dagenham 3, Slough Town 0
Semi-final, second leg	Slough Town 2, Dagenham 3
Final (at Wembley)	Scarborough 2, Dagenham 1

1977/78

First round	Harrow Borough 0, Dagenham 1
Second round	Dagenham 4, Crook Town 2
Third round	Walthamstow Avenue 0, Dagenham 1
Fourth round	Spennymoor United 1, Dagenham 0

Mossley players warm up for training, kitted up for the big day.

1978/79

First round	Dagenham 1, Tooting & Mitcham United 1
First-round replay	Tooting & Mitcham United 0, Dagenham 0
First round, second replay (at Hayes)	Dagenham 3, Tooting & Mitcham United 1
Second round	Witney Town 0, Dagenham 2
Third round	Witton Albion 1, Dagenham 1
Third-round replay	Dagenham 1, Witton Albion 1
Third round, second replay (at Kidderminster)	Dagenham 3, Witton Albion 1
Quarter-final	Dagenham 2, Yeovil Town 0
Semi-final, first leg	Dagenham 0, Kettering Town 0
Semi-final, second leg	Kettering Town 1, Dagenham 0

1979/80

First round	Dorchester Town 0, Dagenham 1
Second round	Stalybridge Celtic 0, Dagenham 5
Third round	Burton Albion 1, Dagenham 1
Third-round replay	Dagenham 3, Burton Albion 1
Fourth round	Dagenham 3, Nuneaton Borough 2
Semi-final, first leg	Woking 1, Dagenham 3
Semi-final, second leg	Dagenham 4, Woking 1
Final (at Wembley)	Dagenham 2, Mossley 1

Routes to the Final

Dagenham

First round	Dorchester Town 0, Dagenham 1
Second round	Stalybridge Celtic 0, Dagenham 5
Third round	Burton Albion 1, Dagenham 1
Third-round replay	Dagenham 3, Burton Albion 1
Fourth round	Dagenham 3, Nuneaton Borough 2
Semi-final, first leg	Woking 1, Dagenham 3
Semi-final, second leg	Dagenham 4, Woking 1

Mossley

First round	Mossley 3, Spennymoor United 2
Second round	Boston 0, Mossley 0
Second-round replay	Mossley 6, Boston 3
Third round	Altrincham 1, Mossley 5
Fourth round	Mossley 1, Blyth Spartans 1
Fourth-round replay	Blyth Spartans 0, Mossley 2
Semi-final, first leg	Mossley 1, Boston United 1
Semi-final, second leg	Boston United 1, Mossley 2

1981

Bishop's Stortford 1, Sutton United 0
Wembley, 16 May 1981

Bishop's Stortford belied their Isthmian League Division One status by beating Sutton United, thanks to a last-minute goal from Terry Sullivan. It was a fitting climax to an extraordinary feat that saw the Blues not only become the first ever club to capture both the FA Amateur Cup and the FA Trophy, but also the first to win the latter after starting at the preliminary round stage. In doing so, Bishop's Stortford completed an extraordinary 13-match trophy run that began with a win against Spalding United the previous September. It was a season that also saw the Blues win the Isthmian League Division One title.

Stortford's trophy saga seemed set to run on even further and even to a fourteenth tie as the ninetieth minute came up at Wembley. Extra time at least looked a formality, and with several Blues players appearing desperately tired it looked as if the underdogs had had their day.

Then the incredible happened. Dave Brame hoisted over a deep cross from the right and under pressure from former Arsenal star John Radford, Sutton captain John Rains headed across his goal. Sullivan beat the Sutton defence to the ball and, after a moment's hesitation, drove it high into the roof of the net. Sutton's players stared disbelievingly at each other as Sullivan careered away in triumph. The startling suddenness of the goal made the three minutes of injury time a formality, before Stortford captain Dave Blackman stepped up to receive the trophy from Bobby Charlton.

Even though it was the seventy-ninth match of the season for Bishop's Stortford, they began the game full of running. Mike Mitchell, in particular, revelled in the wide spaces of Wembley, causing problems for the right side of Sutton's defence throughout the first half.

Mitchell thrived on a string of subtle passes from Radford, who made his previous Wembley experience tell in the opening stages. It was Radford who had the first clear chance of the game on twenty minutes when Joe Simmonds nodded the ball on, but Sutton 'keeper Dave Collyer turned Radford's shot around the post. Sutton hit back with a counter-attack down the left when Graham Dennis got behind the defence and Micky Stephens hit the bar from the resulting cross. Dennis caused more problems for Stortford moments later as he outpaced the defence, but Terry Moore made a confident save.

Bishop's Stortford began the second half brightly and Radford twice went close but Sutton began to look like a team from one division above as the immensely experienced Larry Pritchard began to pull the strings. The Blues' marathon season was taking its toll, and when Moore and David Brame got in a mix-up, Sutton substitute Ray Sunnocks shot into the side netting. But Moore was the hero when Pritchard burst clear, only for the Stortford 'keeper to snatch the ball from under his feet.

Stortford were toiling when Rick Bradford slipped on the ball and lay on the turf immobilised with cramp, but Roger Avery summoned all his reserves to rob the onrushing Dennis. Not long afterwards came Sullivan's shock winner.

Bishop's Stortford sweeper John Knapman was swift to praise Sutton's contribution, but said that they may have been 'too nice' to win. 'They wished us all the best before the game, which was very friendly of them, but maybe that's

The programme for the semi-final first leg between Dartford and Bishop's Stortford.

the sort of thing that you should leave until after the match,' he said. Stortford manager Trevor Harvey pointed to Mitchell's first-half performance as the platform for victory. 'He really turned the game for us', he said. 'He was demoralising Sutton.'

Bishop's Stortford: Moore, Blackman, Brame, Smith, Bradford, Avery, Sullivan, Knapman, Radford, Simmonds, Mitchell. Substitute: Worrell.

Sutton United: Collyer, Rogers, Green, J. Rains, A. Rains, Stephens, Waldon, Pritchard, Cornwall, Parsons, Dennis. Substitute: Sunnocks.

In Focus
The Marathon Trophy

Bishop's Stortford's trophy triumph was truly the culmination of a marathon effort. Their run from the preliminary round included replays against Bridgend Town and Dagenham but that was nothing compared with events elsewhere in the competition.

In the first round, Netherfield and Bridlington Trinity set a record for cup-tie replays when they played each other seven times – in other words, six replays. After a total of thirteen and a half hours play, Netherfield won 2-0 to go through to the second round. One wonders if match programmes were issued for every game and, if so, what they managed to write about!

However, the cost to both clubs was considerable – a total of £1,800 – and it depleted the finances of Netherfield so much that it effectively caused them to move down into the North-West Counties League Division One in 1982. In addition, for all their efforts, Aylesbury unceremoniously dumped Netherfield out 2-0 in the second round. But Aylesbury were made to pay a forfeit for their ruthlessness. They needed 3 games to dispose of Northwich Victoria in round three before falling to Sutton United – you guessed it, after a replay, at the next stage.

Both Bishop's Stortford and Sutton fielded players in the twilight of marathon careers. John Radford came to Stortford after a career that began at Arsenal in 1963 and took in 481 first-team appearances. After spells at West Ham and Blackburn Rovers, Radford joined the Blues in 1979/80 and was later to manage the club with considerable success.

Stortford goalkeeper Terry Moore had clocked up almost 300 appearances for the Blues by Wembley 1981. In his second spell at the club he played for Stortford in the 1974 Amateur Cup final and is the only player to collect both FA Amateur and FA Trophy cup-winners' medals for the same club. But it would take Radford and Moore's combined total appearances to match the extraordinary Larry Pritchard. Sutton's assistant manager, at Wembley in his testimonial season, racked up 781 appearances for Sutton alone between 1965 and 1984. He went over the 1,200-appearance mark in total, thanks to spells with Epsom & Ewell and Wycombe Wanderers, plus 48 England Amateur caps.

Routes to the Final

Bishop's Stortford

Preliminary round	Bishop's Stortford 3, Spalding United 1
First qualifying round	Chelmsford City 1, Bishop's Stortford 2
Second qualifying round	Bishop's Stortford 2, Kingstonian 0
Third qualifying round	Bishop's Stortford 1, Hendon 0
First round	Bishop's Stortford 1, Bridgend Town 1
First-round replay	Bridgend Town 1, Bishop's Stortford 2
Second round	Dagenham 1, Bishop's Stortford 1
Second-round replay	Bishop's Stortford 3, Dagenham 1
Third round	Bishop's Stortford 3, Alvechurch 2
Fourth round	Bishop's Stortford 4, Worcester City 0
Semi-final, first leg	Dartford 1, Bishop's Stortford 1
Semi-final, second leg	Bishop's Stortford 2, Dartford 1

Sutton United

First round	Woking 0, Sutton United 1
Second round	Sutton United 5, Wycombe Wanderers 0
Third round	Sutton United 2, Bedford Town 0
Fourth round	Sutton United 0, Aylesbury United 0
Fourth-round replay	Aylesbury United 0, Sutton United 1
Semi-final, first leg	Bangor City 2, Sutton United 2
Semi-final, second leg	Sutton United 4, Bangor City 2

1982

Enfield 1, Altrincham 0

Wembley, 15 May 1982

An outlandish goal from Paul Taylor finally broke the deadlock and brought FA Trophy glory to Enfield for the first time. With just six minutes of extra time remaining, the little midfielder swung his boot at the ball fully thirty yards from goal – and watched as it sailed into the top corner of the net. Enfield's delighted players knew there and then that they had sealed victory. They ran from all corners to pile on top of Taylor, and it was several moments before his distinctive permed head reappeared – still wearing a huge grin. 'I couldn't believe it, I've never scored a goal like that before', admitted the twenty-one-year-old. 'When I realised how far out I was I almost decided not to shoot, but in the end I just gave it all I had – and I've never seen a prettier sight.'

It was truly one of the classic goals in Wembley's history, though, as an overall spectacle, the game fell some way short of classic status. A cat-and-mouse duel wore on well into the second half, with the crowd growing increasingly restless, and it was only a spate of goalmouth incidents in extra time – capped by Taylor's strike – that saved the game from being a 0-0 non-event.

It looked as if a no-holds-barred contest was in the offing when Altrincham's Graham Heathcote sent John Tone flying with the first tackle of the afternoon. But that aggressive opening flattered to deceive as the tempo dropped right off. Indeed, in its lowest moments, one could be fooled into thinking that referee Brian Stevens had stopped the game for an infringement. With the temperature at 75°F, wily Altrincham were happy to let Enfield do the legwork and it was Robins 'keeper John Connaughton who was busiest, saving twice from Paul Taylor.

Altrincham relied on breakaway raids and one almost paid off when Graham Heathcote's first-time pass found John Rogers, but John Jacobs comfortably stopped a twenty-yard shot. The Enfield 'keeper, who claimed to be sporting the first

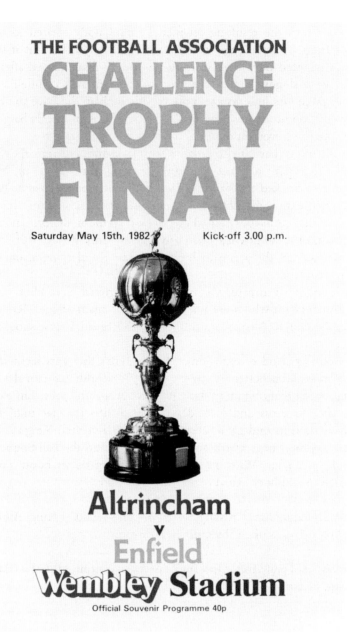

THE FOOTBALL ASSOCIATION

CHALLENGE TROPHY FINAL

Saturday May 15th, 1982   Kick-off 3.00 p.m.

Altrincham
v
Enfield

Wembley Stadium

Official Souvenir Programme 40p

Match programme for 1982 Enfield *v.* Altrincham game.

light-blue shirt to be worn by a goalkeeper in a Wembley final, was in trouble on twenty minutes when he dropped a tricky Barry Howard cross, but recovered to fall on the ball as Jeff Johnson rushed in.

Just before half-time, the game briefly came alight at both ends. First, Nicky Ironton hit a sweet right-footed shot that Connaughton plunged down to palm away for a corner. From the resulting set-piece, Paul Cuddy cleared long to Howard, whose shot from an acute angle was beaten away by Jacobs. But if the spectators' appetite was whetted now, they were to be wholly disappointed after the interval. Both teams were sluggish under the glare of the sun and as Enfield's passing game was lacking, there was little to cheer about. Altrincham did have the ball in the net on seventy-five minutes, but it was disallowed as John King clearly barged Jacobs over the line and did not even raise most Altrincham fans to their feet.

Altrincham might have had the game won five minutes from the end of normal time when Rogers hit a sweet cross to Howard, who, racing in, had too much momentum and cracked the ball over the bar. That seemed to spur Altrincham on and they started extra time with a bang, Howard finding his spot this time only to be remarkably denied. Jacobs rushed out to stop an incoming ball and it spun off his legs straight to Howard, who shot towards an empty net. But Tony Jennings somehow arrived on the scene to head away, before clearing again when Rogers nodded the ball back.

Enfield found fresh impetus when substitute forward Dave Flint was introduced, but it was Altrincham who were within a whisker again when a Rogers header hit the bar and then fell to Altrincham sub Barry Whitbread, whose shot hit Rogers and span away.

In the second period of extra time, Altrincham's thoughts seemed to turn to a possible replay in Manchester – a huge geographical advantage for the Robins – but it was an approach that cost them dear. As they slowed the pace, Enfield's Steve King was easily able to cross and looked set to slip into the net until Ivan Crossley desperately twisted in mid-air to clear the ball for a corner. King's resulting corner was cleared to John Tone, whose shot was blocked and the ball bounced out to the lonely figure of Taylor. With one devastating swing of his boot, Taylor took the trophy back to Southbury Road.

Altrincham: Connaughton, Crossley, Davison, Bailey, Cuddy, King, Allan, Heathcote, Johnson, Rogers, Howard. Substitute: Whitbread.

Enfield: Jacobs, Barrett, Tone, Jennings, Waite, Ironton, Ashfield, Taylor, Holmes, Oliver, King. Substitute: Flint.

In Focus
Enfield – At the Height of Their Powers

Enfield FC is now a broken club, bereft of its much-loved Southbury Road ground, and, at the time of writing, having hauled itself up from the brink of total collapse. It was not always so. In 1982 they were one of non-League's foremost powers and on the brink of the Football League itself. Having reached the fourth round of the FA Cup in 1980/81, Enfield was one of the most talked about clubs outside the League. In 1981/82, when they joined the Alliance Premier League, Enfield finished runners-up to Runcorn, as well as lifting the FA Trophy. They were to win the Alliance the following season.

Ted Hardy, who guided the club to an Isthmian League and Cup double as well as the Middlesex Senior Cup, sowed the seeds of Enfield's success, before Eddie McClusky took over the managerial reins at the end of the 1979/80 season. In 1980/81, Enfield's FA Cup run saw them beat Hereford 2-0 and Port Vale 3-0 in a replay to earn a fourth-round trip to a Barnsley side already earmarked for promotion to Division Two. But Enfield drew 1-1 to take Barnsley back to London, where the replay was held at White Hart Lane in front of an amazing 35,000 crowd. Enfield lost 3-0, but that, plus an Isthmian League runners-up spot, saw them move into the Alliance. Enfield repeated their FA Cup exploits, crushing Wimbledon 4-1 and losing 3-2 to Crystal Palace.

Backed by very efficient administration under the chairmanship of Tommy Unwin, McClusky, who came to Enfield after ten years at Barking, instilled a professionalism that saw his side give everything and practise 'total football.'

McClusky looked for goals from all positions, saying: 'Attacking football can be played through the back four and having four in midfield does not make us a defensive side.' Even goalkeeper John Jacobs converted a penalty. Defenders Keith Barrett, Dave Waite and Tony Jennings all represented the England semi-professional side, the latter as captain.

Nowadays, Enfield and the recently formed Enfield Town both lay claim to this rich heritage, with the latter club in the Essex Senior League. It is to be hoped that long-suffering fans in both camps can one day see glory days return.

Routes to the Final

Altrincham

First round	Altrincham 1, Nuneaton Borough 0
Second round	Epsom & Ewell 0, Altrincham 1
Third round	Altrincham 2, Mossley 0
Fourth round	Altrincham 2, Bishop's Stortford 2
Fourth-round replay	Bishop's Stortford 1, Altrincham 3
Semi-final, first leg	Altrincham 1, Wycombe Wanderers 1
Semi-final, second leg	Wycombe Wanderers 0, Altrincham 3

Enfield

First round	Weymouth 0, Enfield 1
Second round	Merthyr Tydfil 1, Enfield 6
Third round	Telford United 0, Enfield 1
Fourth round	Enfield 4, Scarborough 2
Semi-final, first leg	Northwich Victoria 0, Enfield 0
Semi-final, second leg	Enfield 1, Northwich Victoria 0

1983

Telford United 2, Northwich Victoria 1
Wembley, 14 May 1983

Non-League goal-machine Dave Mather sealed Telford's second FA Trophy win with two superb opportunist goals that sank Northwich. Mather, who joined Telford from Bangor City in 1980, carved a reputation as one of the most dangerous strikers outside the Football League, netting 37 times in 1981/82. He did not disappoint on the big day.

His first goal, just forty seconds after the half-time interval, showed his lethal knack of taking chances. Chesting down a Colin Williams flick, Mather unleashed a left-footed shot from six yards that gave Northwich 'keeper Dave Ryan no chance. Mather said, 'It was chest high and I swung my foot at it and caught it perfectly. Rhino (Dave Ryan) is still looking for it now.'

Mather's second goal, in the seventieth minute, was a piece of pure opportunism. Williams was again the provider, this time showing great flair to flick the ball over the head of Northwich captain Ken Jones, before hammering a shot that Ryan could only parry straight into the path of Mather – who finished the job with his head.

That goal sealed the trophy for Telford during a spell in which they dominated, showing more of the control that had been missing from a scrappy first forty-five minutes. The first half was, however, anything but dull. Mather shot just wide with a shot on the run in the fourth minute and seven minutes later Paul Reid almost made the most of a Steve Eaton stumble at the other end, but Telford 'keeper Kevin Charlton came out to tackle bravely on the edge of the area. Dave Barnett missed a chance to put Telford ahead when he fired a John Alcock cross straight at Ryan, who later had to deal with a powerful Paul Mayman header from the effective Alcock.

Northwich matched Telford, with Charlton kept busy to collect a John Anderson cross and Alan Walker putting in a well-timed tackle to foil Reid. But Telford took a grip on the game in the first twenty-five minutes of the second-half, when Northwich

Defeat — but what a day to remember in 1983

● A magic moment as Ken Jones exchanges pennants before the kick off.

● A 'Fan-cy' dresser

● Triumphant Telford

● A 1983 Wembley special

● Mark Ward's misery

lost their way and rarely made it forward. It was only when Telford had gone 2-0 up that Northwich showed what they could do – and though they made Telford sweat, it was just too late. Charlton had to punch clear from both Colin Chesters and substitute Paul Bennett, and it was the latter who put Vics back in with a shout with fifteen minutes remaining. Mark Ward sent over a cross that was flicked on by Phil Wilson and Bennett struck with a scissors kick that Charlton could only palm into the net.

It was all hands to the pump for Telford and Charlton saved them three minutes later with a brilliant arching stop, to prevent Reid equalising with a back header from Wilson's long throw. Northwich pressed to the last without finding a way through, in a tumultuous last few minutes that reflected the hard but fair spirit in which the game was played. Having collected their trophy and medals, the Telford players waited to a man to commiserate with their opponents.

Telford boss Stan Storton said, 'I am sorry we had to beat Northwich because I have so many friends there. It was nice of them to come up to us at the end and say that they did not mind losing if they lost to us.' Northwich manager John King admitted, 'I'm not going to say Telford were not the better side. For twenty minutes in the second half they played some magic football. I have a very good team but so have they. All credit to Telford; they put it together better than we did.'

Telford United: Charlton, Lewis, Turner, Mayman, Walker, Eaton, Barnett, Williams, Mather, Hogan, Alcock. Substitute: Joseph.

Northwich Victoria: Ryan, Fretwell, Murphy, Jones, Forshaw, Ward, Anderson, Abel, Reid, Chesters, Wilson. Substitute: Bennett.

Opposite: Montage of photographs from a special publication released for Northwich Victoria's FA Trophy final appearance.

Right: Match programme for the 1983 FA Trophy final.

In Focus
Trophies All Day and Night for Telford

Saturday 14 May was a day of celebration and trophies for Telford. It began with the big one in the afternoon but went on into the same evening before the celebrations continued long into the night. A reception at the team's Wembley hotel saw midfielder Eddie Hogan, already voted the player of the year by the club's travelling fans, roundly cheered by around twenty members of his family, who made the trip from Ireland to see him play and then collect the players' player of the year trophy. Hogan, who returned to Telford in January 1981 after a brief spell at Nuneaton, was the driving force behind Telford's FA Trophy run, with 3 goals.

Defender Steve Eaton was voted the most improved player of the year, while Dave Mather picked up his third successive award as the season's leading goalscorer.

Manager Stan Storton nominated Kevin Charlton for a new award for the best individual performance of the season. Charlton made a string of crucial saves throughout the season, including in the semi-final second leg at Harrow, where Telford stormed through in extra time to win 5-1 and 5-3 on aggregate. But his award came for an epic display at Wigan Athletic in the first round of the FA Cup that gave Telford a replay and eventually a place in the second round.

Routes to the Final

Northwich Victoria

First round	Kidderminster Harriers 0, Northwich Victoria 3
Second round	Northwich Victoria 1, Croydon 0
Third round	Northwich Victoria 1, Bangor City 1
Third-round replay	Bangor City 2, Northwich Victoria 2
Third round, second replay (at Wrexham)	Northwich Victoria 1, Bangor City 0
Fourth round	Blyth Spartans 1, Northwich Victoria 1
Fourth-round replay	Northwich Victoria 3, Blyth Spartans 2
Semi-final, first leg	Northwich Victoria 3, Dagenham 2
Semi-final, second leg	Dagenham 0, Northwich Victoria 1

Telford United

First round	Burton Albion 0, Telford United 1
Second round	Spennymoor United 0, Telford United 0
Second-round replay	Telford United 2, Spennymoor United 1
Third round	Telford United 3, Scarborough 0
Fourth round	Telford United 4, Dartford 0
Semi-final, first leg	Telford United 0, Harrow Borough 2
Semi-final, second leg	Harrow Borough 1, Telford United 5

1984

Northwich Victoria 1, Bangor City 1
Wembley, 12 May 1984

For the second successive year Northwich froze on the big day at Wembley – but this time they were given a reprieve. When both sets of players wearily trudged off the Wembley turf after their 120-minute London marathon – the first draw in fifteen FA Trophy finals – it was Vics who were luckiest to have lived to fight another day. With just five minutes of extra time remaining, Bangor captain Mark Carter was presented with a wonderful opportunity to take the trophy back to Wales. Sent racing clear by his co-striker Ian Howat, he picked his spot with a low shot from ten yards out. For a split second the Vics faced defeat, but goalkeeper Dave Ryan flung himself high and wide to pull off the most important save of his life.

The mantle of favourites proved too heavy for manager John King's men, as underdogs Bangor produced most of the positive action. All the forecasts said Vics would cash in on experience gained from the previous season's defeat to Telford United. The reality was very different, as they did not force a single corner during the entire 120 minutes.

Colin Chesters battled hard for the Vics and Paul Reid ran himself into the ground chasing lost causes as Northwich's midfield failed to fire. It took the introduction of seventeen-year-old Phil Power to light the Vics' fire. It was no surprise, therefore, when Bangor took the lead in the fifty-eighth minute. Vics skipper Ken Jones, playing his 900th game for the club, made his only mistake of the afternoon in allowing Carter to get behind him. The ex-South Liverpool striker, who was playing with a broken wrist, kept his head in squaring for Tony Whelan to hammer the ball high into the net.

King threw on Power for the injured Jeff Forshaw and he quickly made his mark in preventing Bruce Urquhart from making it 2-0. Then Mark Dean, the only Vics starter not in the previous year's defeated team, combined with Chesters to rescue Northwich. Dean skipped past two defenders and smartly sidestepped referee John Martin before curling a cross over Bangor 'keeper Glen Letheren for Chesters, who showed his quality finishing in diving full-length to head in the equaliser. Then the strength-sapping Wembley pitch took its toll in extra time. Jones called upon all his experience to keep the Vics together while Bangor boss Dave Elliott played his last card in throwing on sub Kevin Westwood. But it was Ryan who ensured that both sides had to head to Stoke to do it all again.

Northwich Victoria: Ryan, Fretwell, Jones, Forshaw, Dean, Wilson, Abel, Bennett, Anderson, Chesters, Reid. Substitute: Power.

Bangor City: Letheren, Cavanagh, Banks, Lunn, Gray, Urquhart, Morris, Whelan, Sutcliffe, Howat, Carter. Substitute: Westwood.

Northwich Victoria 2, Bangor City 1
Victoria Ground, Stoke, 15 May 1984

Three years of FA Trophy battling erupted into ecstatic celebrations as the Vics clinched the greatest prize in their history just ten seconds before the final whistle. The hero for Northwich in the first ever trophy-final replay was winger John Anderson with a dramatic goal, as everyone in the stadium prepared themselves for extra time. Anderson cracked the ball through 'keeper Glen Letheren's legs to hand Northwich manager John King the crown that his inspiration merited.

After Anderson's goal there was barely time for referee John Martin to blow his whistle for the restart before the Welshmen were counted out and Northwich skipper Ken Jones lifted the trophy on his 901st appearance. It was cruel on Bangor, but Northwich showed great character to come from a goal behind. In a rugged game, the tally of five bookings and forty-eight free-kicks only reflected the players' commitment. The match was not one for purists, Northwich again struggling to create chances, but the atmosphere was intense in the closer surroundings of Stoke's Victoria Ground. A notable difference from Wembley was that Northwich's midfield worked tirelessly to harass their Bangor opponents to distraction.

Nevertheless, it was once again Bangor who took the lead on eighteen minutes. A free-kick saw Alan Morris tap the ball to defender Phil Lunn, who crashed a low twenty-yard drive past 'keeper Dave Ryan. A clear penalty decision ten minutes before the break saw the Vics draw level. It was awarded when Bruce Urquhart palmed down a header from Phil Wilson. Saturday's scorer Colin Chesters scored with precision from the spot.

The second half looked to be little to write home about until the dying seconds, when Wilson and Graham Abel combined in a final thrust. Paul Bennett then nodded the ball behind the Bangor defence to give Anderson his chance to earn his place in Northwich's hall of fame. Northwich boss John King later admitted, 'John Anderson's play before his goal was almost embarrassing and I did think about making a substitution. But John is just the sort of player to suddenly do something special and I decided to save Phil Power for extra time.'

Northwich Victoria: Ryan, Fretwell, Jones, Forshaw, Dean, Bennett, Abel, Wilson, Anderson, Chesters, Reid. Substitute: Power.

Bangor City: Letheren, Cavanagh, Banks, Lunn, Gray, Urquhart, Morris, Whelan, Sutcliffe, Carter, Howat. Substitute: Westwood.

In Focus
A Welsh Club Reaches Wembley after Fifty-Seven Years

(With thanks to Bangor City's historical website)
Bangor City had very little time to indulge in celebration or anticipation at becoming the first Welsh club to reach Wembley since 1927. As well as reaching the final of English non-League football's premier cup competition, they had also had a great run in the FA Cup, reaching the second round proper where they faced Blackpool, taking the full-timers to a replay that City narrowly lost. Meanwhile, City were in their second season in the Alliance Premier League but were struggling to avoid the drop back down to the Northern Premier League.

Unfortunately for City, their successful cup runs had left them with a huge backlog of league fixtures. In the two weeks between the FA Trophy semi-final and the final itself, City were forced to play no less than 10 league games, 5 of which were lost, thereby condemning them to the drop. Some Alliance Premier League clubs appeared to be reluctant to rearrange the games, postponed due to cup commitments, while City were playing well, and this was the reason that manager Dave Elliott insisted was responsible for City arriving at Wembley's Twin Towers having been relegated.

Whatever sense of disappointment City fans had felt was made up for by the sense of occasion of playing at Wembley against Northwich Victoria. Two trains packed full of City supporters were specially laid on for the trip down to London, and in total around 7,000 fans travelled by whatever means they could. A crowd of over 14,500 turned out at Wembley to see the two teams presented before the match to former England manager Ron Greenwood CBE.

Paul Whelan was the first, and only, City player ever to score at Wembley in the 1-1 draw. The replay was held at the Victoria Ground, Stoke, and due to its close proximity to Northwich, City officials and supporters felt it gave their opponents an unfair advantage. Although City fans still turned out in force for the replay, they were greatly outnumbered by the Northwich Victoria fans, who only had to make a short journey down the road to cheer their team on.

It was the last season that City were to play in the English non-League top flight, although they came close to returning there in 1987 when they finished as Multipart Northern Premier League runners-up.

Match programme for the Bangor City v. Northwich Victoria FA Trophy final replay, Tuesday 15 May 1984.

Routes to the Final

Northwich Victoria

First round	Boston United 1, Northwich Victoria 1
First-round replay	Northwich Victoria 5, Boston United 1
Second round	Aylesbury United 0, Northwich Victoria 1
Third round	Dulwich Hamlet 0, Northwich Victoria 0
Third-round replay	Northwich Victoria 0, Dulwich Hamlet 0
Third round, second replay (at Nuneaton)	Northwich Victoria 1, Dulwich Hamlet 0
Fourth round	Northwich Victoria 1, Barnet 0
Semi-final, first leg	Northwich Victoria 1, Marine 1
Semi-final, second leg	Marine 0, Northwich Victoria 2

Bangor City

First round	Bangor City 3, Spennymoor United 1
Second round	Bangor City 1, Bath City 0
Third round	Gateshead 2, Bangor City 2
Third-round replay	Bangor City 2, Gateshead 0
Fourth round	AP Leamington 1, Bangor City 6
Semi-final, first leg	Bangor City 1, Dagenham 0
Semi-final, second leg	Dagenham 2, Bangor City 2

1985

Wealdstone 2, Boston United 1
Wembley, 11 May 1985

Wealdstone raced out of the traps to beat battling Boston and become the first team to win the Conference and FA Trophy double. Playing as well as they had done all season, Wealdstone ran Boston ragged in the first half, and although the Pilgrims came back strongly after the interval they could not claw back a two-goal deficit. Wealdstone got off to a flyer when Andy Graham scored with a stunning overhead kick from a corner after just eighty-four seconds. Brian Greenaway floated the ball in to Graham, who flicked it up in the air, half turned to goal and then hooked the ball over his shoulder and past the despairing dive of Boston 'keeper Kevin Blackwell.

Wealdstone looked sharp, knocked the ball about confidently and accurately and gave Boston no breathing space. Left-back Roy Davies began several attacks down his side, Greenaway was busy on the other flank, Alan Cordice and Graham were a danger all along the front line and United were on the rack. Wealdstone looked certain to go further ahead on nineteen minutes when Ray O'Brien conceded a penalty after using his hand to stop a Paul Bowgett header going into the net. Dennis Byatt hammered a right-foot kick that arrowed towards the bottom corner. But Blackwell guessed correctly and pulled off a magnificent save by flinging himself to his left to push the ball around the post.

The Pilgrims' luck couldn't last much longer. On twenty-eight minutes Wealdstone extended their lead from another Greenaway corner. His kick found an unmarked Lee Holmes rising on the penalty spot to send a powerful header that shot fiercely off Ian Ladd or Graham, or both, and into the roof of the net. Wealdstone looked to have done enough to be home and hosed, but they were sent on the back foot by a Boston fightback straight after the interval. Boston skipper Gary Simpson finally began to find his midfield game and poked a ball that Wealdstone 'keeper Bob Iles just beat Chris Cook to. Thirty seconds later, Simpson put in a deep cross that had Bob Lee lining up a shot before full-back Steve Perkins raced over to hoof the ball off his toe.

The warning shots had been fired and on forty-nine minutes Boston got the goal that they were desperate for. It was Paul Casey who provided a through ball to Cook and the blond striker beat defender Byatt and 'keeper Iles to send the ball over the line. Wealdstone suddenly looked rattled, and Ian Ladd and Brian Thomson both had chances that went wide. Wealdstone, meanwhile, only had Alan Cordice forward but were dangerous on the break. On seventy-four minutes Wealdstone had the ball in the net, but Gary Donnellan was penalised for flattening Blackwell as he was about to catch a dropping ball.

Five minutes from time Boston thought they had snatched the elusive goal when Dave Gilbert poked the ball home, but it was ruled out for offside. The linesman had long been flagging and there could be no real complaints. Wealdstone held on and the statistics showed that it had truly been a final of two halves. In the first half, Wealdstone had six shots on target and three that missed; Boston had no shots on target and five off target. In the second half, Boston had two shots on target and another five off target. Wealdstone had no attempts – on or off target. Boston had three corners – Wealdstone had six, five of them in the first forty-five minutes.

Boston United: Blackwell, Casey, Ladd, Creane, O'Brien, Thomson, Laverick, Simpson, Gilbert, Lee, Cook. Substitute: Mallender.

Wealdstone: Iles, Perkins, Davies, Byatt, Bowgett, Wainwright, Greenaway, Holmes, A. Cordice, Graham, Donnellan. Substitute: N. Cordice.

In Focus
Wealdstone's Wembley Wonders

Wealdstone manager Brian Hall built a superbly balanced side to win the Conference (then Gola League) and FA Trophy double. A police physical training instructor who played as a centre half for the Metropolitan Police, Hall came to Wealdstone in 1983, having previously worked at Wimbledon. After Wealdstone, he went on to manage Yeovil Town. Sadly, he died of cancer in 1999, aged just fifty-nine.

Hall coached an uncompromising direct style of football and was a good organiser, skilled at building a successful side with limited resources. A believer that any successful side must be built on a solid defence, Hall had no worries between the posts with Bob Iles in goal, a former England Youth representative who played 14 first team games for Chelsea. Right full-back at Wembley was the experienced Steve Perkins, who joined Wealdstone in 1981 having earlier played 52 Football League games for Wimbledon. On the other side of the field was Roy Davies, another former Wimbledon player who also had experience at Reading and Torquay United. The rock of defence was completed in the middle with captain Paul Bowgett, another ex-Wimbledon name and an England semi-professional

Above: Wealdstone's Wembley walk. From left to right: Roy Davies, Nigel Johnson, Dennis Byatt, Robin Wainwright and Vinnie Jones in a pre-match publicity shot.

Right: Wealdstone's smartly kitted out squad pose before heading off to Wembley.

international, and powerful centre half Dennis Byatt, formerly of Northampton Town. The pair was probably Wealdstone's best ever central defensive partnership.

Pulling the strings in midfield was the wise old head of Robin Wainwright, the thirty-four-year-old being in his sixth season at Wealdstone, with his former clubs including Northampton Town, Luton, Cambridge United and Millwall. It was a class act in the middle of the park as he was joined by Brian Greenaway, a Hall signing in the summer of 1984 from Fulham, where he made 85 appearances on the wing. Wembley scorer Lee Holmes completed the midfield trio, having been signed from Dartford at the beginning of the season.

Hall's most inspired signing, in October 1984, was Andy Graham from Lancaster City, where he had scored 26 goals in 51 games. A natural goalscorer, he had the uncanny knack, as he showed in spectacular style at Wembley, of scoring with his back to goal. Graham's other goals included the only strike in a win at Kettering to seal the Gola League Championship. Up front with Graham were former Reading player Andy Donnellan and speedy striker Alan Cordice, who boasted six England semi-professional caps at the time. Cordice's brother Neil, also a forward and in his fifth season at Wealdstone, was on the substitutes' bench. Neil was sometimes overshadowed by his older brother but was one of Wealdstone's most loyal players, racking up over 500 first-team appearances.

One player who got only a brief mention in the Wembley programme and did not play, was one Vinnie Jones, or Vince Jones, as he was described there. A labourer, plucked by Hall from Sunday League football obscurity, Jones spent two seasons as a bit-part player at Wealdstone before Dave Bassett swooped for the hard man in a surprise £10,000 deal to take him to Wimbledon. Hence, without Hall and Bassett, it is most unlikely that Jones would have trodden the unlikely path from Wealdstone to Welsh international football and Hollywood film stardom.

Routes to the Final

Boston United

Third qualifying round	Alvechurch 1, Boston United 2
First round	Boston United 5, Blyth Spartans 4
Second round	Boston United 4, Frome Town 0
Third round	Boston United 1, Wokingham Town 0
Fourth round	Boston United 3, Runcorn 0
Semi-final, first leg	Altrincham 0, Boston United 0
Semi-final, second leg	Boston United 3, Altrincham 2

Wealdstone

First round	Harlow Town 0, Wealdstone 0
First-round replay	Wealdstone 5, Harlow Town 0
Second round	Wealdstone 2, Wycombe Wanderers 1
Third round	Wealdstone 3, Welling United 1
Fourth round	Wealdstone 3, Frickley Athletic 1
Semi-final, first leg	Enfield 0, Wealdstone 2
Semi-final, second leg	Wealdstone 0, Enfield 1

1986

Altrincham 1, Runcorn 0
Wembley, 17 May 1986

Mike Farrelly's first non-League cup goal was enough to sink Runcorn and bring the FA Trophy back to Moss Lane for the second time in eight years. Thoughts on the pitch and on the terraces were turning to half-time when, at 3.43 p.m., Phil Gardner gathered the ball in the centre circle. He took a couple of paces forwards, glanced up and with his left foot sent Gary Anderson scampering down the right wing.

The Runcorn defence was caught frighteningly square as Anderson took the ball neatly, stopped, flicked it past a desperately scrambling defender and crossed. Farrelly met the ball true at waist height on the first bounce. His shot hit the underside of the crossbar and for a moment it appeared that the ball was going to bounce out, but the unmistakable rippling net sent the Robins fans into raptures. It was a special moment for a man whose previous Wembley appearances had been on the terraces watching Manchester City.

Farrelly's decider was one of just two clear chances in ninety minutes marred by a slippery Wembley turf and Runcorn's inability to muster a shot once they reached Altrincham's eighteen-yard area. The other came just two minutes after the goal, as referee Tony Ward was about to blow for half-time. Ronnie Ellis' cross, hit hard and low from the left, fell perfectly for Jeff Johnson. The grey-haired defender was quick to side-foot goalwards, but Runcorn's Ray McBride saved spectacularly to his right.

In the event, Farrelly's touch of class was enough. Runcorn fell victim to Wembley nerves – 'We didn't play at all', admitted their manager John Williams. 'Altrincham deserved it.' Indeed, Altrincham 'keeper Jeff Wealand's eighteen-year dream to play at Wembley was so uneventful that the former Manchester United man had not a single shot to save, and filled in his time taking high aimless balls from Runcorn's wingers. The dying minutes were, as ever, frantic, but Altrincham never looked like letting go of a firm grip on the trophy.

Altrincham manager John King, the first man to win the trophy first as a player and then as a manager, said, 'We put in a very competent, very professional performance and it's great to bring the trophy back to Moss Lane – especially to show the people who said we wouldn't win.' Altrincham chairman Gerry Berman added, 'It gives everyone at the club a great kick to win – but now there will be an all-out effort to win the big one: promotion to the League next season.'

Goal-hero Farrelly missed his moment of glory. 'I didn't see it go in', admitted the former Preston defender, who was knocked over as his shot hit the target. 'I heard it hit the bar and the next thing I knew I was mobbed by the lads.' Farrelly came down to earth with more mundane things on his mind. 'Now I'm going to look for a job,' he concluded.

Altrincham: Wealands, Gardner, Densmore, Johnson, Farrelly, Conning, Cuddy, Davison, Reid, Ellis, Anderson. Substitute: Newton.

Runcorn: McBride, Lee, Roberts, Jones, Fraser, Smith, S. Crompton, Imrie, Carter, Mather, Carrodus. Substitute: A. Crompton.

In Focus
Altrincham's Trophy Decade

Altrincham's 1986 FA Trophy triumph capped a ten-year period in which they proved one of the dominant clubs in the competition. Not only did they reach three finals, winning two, but also made it to the semi-finals on three occasions, including in 1977, when they only fell to eventual winners Scarborough after a second replay. The other four years consisted of one quarter-final, twice getting into the third round, and twice being eliminated in the first round.

Altrincham's FA Trophy record, 1976/77-1985/86:

1976/77

Third qualifying round	Altrincham 3, Buxton 1
First round	Altrincham 2, Winsford United 1
Second round	Altrincham 2, Atherstone Town 0
Third round	Altrincham 1, Matlock Town 0
Fourth round	Weymouth 0, Altrincham 0
Fourth-round replay	Altrincham 2, Weymouth 1
Semi-final, first leg	Scarborough 2, Altrincham 0
Semi-final, second leg	Altrincham 2, Scarborough 0
Semi-final replay (at Rotherham)	Altrincham 0, Scarborough 0
Semi-final, second replay (at Doncaster)	Scarborough 2, Altrincham 1

1977/78

First round	Workington 0, Altrincham 0
First-round replay	Altrincham 4, Workington 0
Second round	Altrincham 4, Frickley Athletic 0
Third round	Matlock Town 1, Altrincham 1
Third-round replay	Altrincham 2, Matlock Town 0
Fourth round	Altrincham 4, Winsford United 2
Semi-final, first leg	Altrincham 0, Runcorn 0
Semi-final, second leg	Runcorn 0, Altrincham 1
Final (at Wembley)	Altrincham 3, Leatherhead 1

1978/79

First round	Altrincham 1, Cheltenham Town 2

1979/80

First round	Grantham 1, Altrincham 1
First-round replay	Altrincham 6, Grantham 3
Second round	Altrincham 2, Morecambe 0
Third round	Altrincham 1, Mossley 5

THE FOOTBALL ASSOCIATION

CHALLENGE TROPHY FINAL

Saturday 17th May, 1986 Kick-off 3.00 p.m.

Altrincham

Runcorn

Wembley

The 1986 match programme, for Altrincham *v.* Runcorn.

1980/81

First round	Altrincham 3, Spennymoor United 2
Second round	Winsford United 0, Altrincham 2
Third round	Leytonstone and Ilford 0, Altrincham 1
Fourth round	Dartford 3, Altrincham 1

1981/82

First round	Altrincham 1, Nuneaton Borough 0
Second round	Epsom & Ewell 0, Altrincham 1
Third round	Altrincham 2, Mossley 0
Fourth round	Altrincham 2, Bishop's Stortford 2
Quarter-final replay	Bishop's Stortford 1, Altrincham 3
Semi-final, first leg	Altrincham 1, Wycombe Wanderers 1
Semi-final, second leg	Wycombe Wanderers 0, Altrincham 3
Final (at Wembley)	Enfield 1, Altrincham 0

1982/83

First round	Corby Town 1, Altrincham 1
First-round replay	Altrincham 6, Corby Town 0
Second round	Tow Law Town 2, Altrincham 2
Second-round replay	Altrincham 3, Tow Law Town 0
Third round	Blyth Spartans 2, Altrincham 0

1983/84

First round	Altrincham 0, Kidderminster Harriers 2

1984/85

First round	Morecambe 0, Altrincham 2
Second round	Burton Albion 1, Altrincham 2
Third round	Altrincham 2, Bishop Auckland 1
Fourth round	Altrincham 4, Stafford Rangers 1
Semi-final, first leg	Altrincham 0, Boston United 0
Semi-final, second leg	Boston United 3, Altrincham 2

1985/86

First round	Ryhope Community Association 1, Altrincham 3
Second round	Altrincham 6, Bangor City 1
Third round	Altrincham 1, Bishop Auckland 0

Fourth round	Cheltenham Town 0, Altrincham 2
Semi-final, first leg	Enfield 1, Altrincham 1
Semi-final, second leg	Altrincham 2, Enfield 0
Final (at Wembley)	Altrincham 1, Runcorn 0

Routes to the Final

Altrincham

First round	Ryhope Community Association 1, Altrincham 3
Second round	Altrincham 6, Bangor City 1
Third round	Altrincham 1, Bishop Auckland 0
Fourth round	Cheltenham Town 0, Altrincham 2
Semi-final, first leg	Enfield 1, Altrincham 1
Semi-final, second leg	Altrincham 2, Enfield 0

Runcorn

First round	Runcorn 2, Marine 0
Second round	Windsor & Eton 0, Runcorn 1
Third round	Runcorn 2, Burton Albion 0
Fourth round	Kidderminster Harriers 1, Runcorn 2
Semi-final, first leg	Runcorn 0, Kettering Town 0
Semi-final, second leg	Kettering Town 0, Runcorn 2

1987

Burton Albion 0, Kidderminster Harriers 0
Wembley, 9 May 1987

Burton Albion belied their underdog status by matching Kidderminster Harriers and forcing an FA Trophy final replay after a stamina-sapping 0-0 draw at Wembley. Conference side Kidderminster, a club with Football League aspirations, started the game to script. Indeed, if they could have found the net during the first twenty minutes, the event could have followed the expected storyline. Adrian O'Dowd fired a long-range shot wide in the first minute and star striker Kim Casey shot over in the opening exchanges. Albion recovered to win a corner after seven minutes, but it was Kidderminster who had the best early chance soon after, with Burton 'keeper Martin New forced into a fine double save from Micky Tuohy and Casey.

Burton began to find their feet and should have taken the lead on thirty-three minutes. Winger Neil Dorsett's centre found Bob Gauden unmarked, but the striker hesitated and O'Dowd was able to clear. Four minutes later a poor back pass from Colin Brazier set Dave Redfern clear for the Brewers. His shot beat 'keeper Jim Arnold but went wide.

Burton continued in confident mood after the interval, with Gil Land twice shooting wide of the target. Casey continued to look the most dangerous player for Kidderminster, notably when cutting in to the Burton penalty area, but lacking direction with his shot. Burton forced a succession of corners and Land had a shot tipped over, but it was Kidderminster who nearly grabbed the winner in the closing minutes of normal time. Burton sweeper Alan Kamara, showing why he would go on to play in the Football League with a sterling performance, cleared off the line from Tuohy before Harriers' striker Paul Davies, who would be the scourge of Albion in the second match, hit the underside of the bar. Davies then shot wide when it looked easier to score after New dropped the ball, as the Brewers fans held their breath.

In extra time, as the sun beat down on Wembley, Kidderminster appeared to wilt but the Burton players seemed to find fresh reserves, thanks perhaps to an 'electrolyte cocktail' served up to the Brewers players by the team doctor. The cocktail was a healthy mixture of salts, sugar and glucose, to help retain fluids and keep tired limbs going. Harriers boss Graham Allner, on the other hand, had to scream at his players to stay on their feet during the interval before extra time.

Paul Groves, Dave Redfern and Gauden all had chances to score as the Brewers pushed forward and Allner admitted he was happy to hear the final whistle. 'I was disappointed that our game started to slip after such a tremendous start', he said. 'However, I don't think the spectators realised just how hot it was out there for the lads. It was bad enough in the dugout but even worse on the turf.' Both sides went up the Wembley steps together, and received a standing ovation. It was generally agreed that a draw was a very fair result and it was now down to the respective managers to try and lift their players for another ninety minutes of effort the following Tuesday.

Burton Albion: New, Kamara, Simms, Vaughan, Essex, Land, Groves, Bancroft, Gauden, Redfern, Dorsett. Substitutes: Wood, Patterson.

Kidderminster Harriers: Arnold, Barton, Collins, Boxall, Brazier, Woodall, McKenzie, Casey, Davies, Tuohy, O'Dowd. Substitutes: Pearson, Jones.

Kidderminster Harriers 2, Burton Albion 1
The Hawthorns, 12 May 1987

While Wembley was a tense match and great day out for Kidderminster and Burton fans, the replay at West Bromwich the following Tuesday was far better in terms of drama, excitement and atmosphere. Although there were less people watching than at Wembley, the closer confines of The Hawthorns on a damp spring evening made for a much more intense atmosphere for those making up West Brom's biggest crowd of that season – 15,685. The replay also had what was missing at Wembley – goals. And, but for some ill luck, the final tally could have favoured Burton.

Indeed, Albion found the net after just ninety seconds. Bob Gauden beat Jim Arnold with a header that went in off the post, but his goal was disallowed, referee Don Shaw deeming that he had climbed on Colin Brazier. Harriers had to deal with long periods of pressure from Albion, and Neil Dorsett, who had delayed his return to New Zealand football to play in the match, was a constant torment to John Barton down the left flank. However, it was Kidderminster who made the vital breakthrough in the thirty-first minute. Striker Paul Davies' low shot took a cruel deflection off Alan Kamara to leave Albion 'keeper Martin New wrong-footed.

Burton came out in the second half attacking the Birmingham Road Kop, where their supporters were massed, and, roared on by the travelling army, continued to

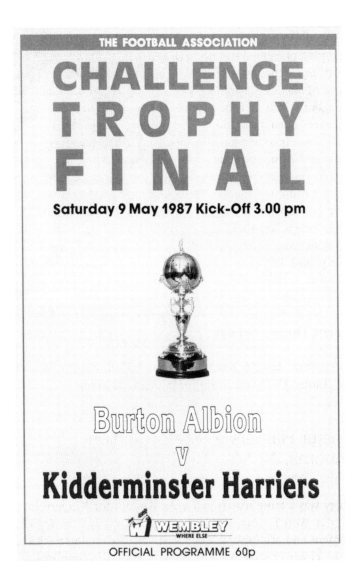

Programme for the 1987 FA Trophy final between Burton Albion and Kidderminster Harriers.

surge forward. But all their possession could not produce the goal they strived so hard for, and the Brewers' hard work seemed to have been in vain when Harriers made it 2-0 on seventy-eight minutes, Davies again the scorer after breaking free.

Far from being disheartened, Burton dug even deeper and within a minute they were back in the game, Paul Groves leaping above the Harriers defence to head in a cross from skipper David Vaughan. With just four minutes left on the clock, Kidderminster defender Graham McKenzie handled inside his own area. Yet another thirty minutes of extra time looked on the cards as Paul Bancroft, influential throughout both games and an assured penalty taker, stepped up to place the ball on

BURTON ALBION VERSUS

KIDDERMINSTER HARRIERS

The
Hawthorns
West
Bromwich

Tuesday
12th May
1987
Kick-off:
7·30 pm

F.A. CHALLENGE TROPHY FINAL REPLAY

● PRICE: 60p
Official Programme

Programme for the 1987 FA Trophy final replay played at Hawthorns.

the spot. But, despite a firm spot kick, Harriers 'keeper Arnold guessed correctly which way Bancroft would shoot, and got down to tip the ball round his right-hand post. Burton had no more to give and the trophy was Kidderminster's.

Burton Albion: New, Kamara, Simms, Vaughan, Essex, Land, Groves, Bancroft, Gauden, Redfern, Dorsett. Substitutes: Wood, Patterson.

Kidderminster Harriers: Arnold, Barton, Collins, Boxall, Brazier, Woodall, McKenzie, Casey, Davies, Tuohy, O'Dowd. Substitutes: Hazelwood, Pearson.

In Focus
Fidler Calls the Tune Again

Burton manager Brian Fidler already had a place in FA Trophy history, having scored the first ever goal in a final as Macclesfield Town defeated Telford United 2-0 in 1970. Sixteen years later, he led Burton Albion to one of the greatest days in their history; but for a few favourable results around October 1986, he might have been relegated to a mere footnote in Burton history. Fidler had graduated to the assistant's post at Burton after successful spells at Frecheville CA – who he took to the quarter-finals of the FA Vase – and Gainsborough Trinity.

At Burton, he assisted manager Neil Warnock in the club's extraordinary FA Cup run to the third round in 1985, where they twice lost to Leicester City after the first match was ordered to be replayed behind closed doors following crowd disturbances. When Warnock resigned in March 1986, before going on to steer Scarborough into the Football League, Fidler – the man who had put an end to Burton's trophy hopes as a Macclesfield player seventeen years before – was given the job on a caretaker and then permanent basis.

Fidler had a tough baptism, as Burton's Albion's 1986/87 campaign got off to a terrible start – they won only 3 games out of 14 in the Northern Premier League, and Fidler clung on to his job by the skin of his teeth. Money was tight and Fidler had to try and improve his squad with young players brought in from local football alongside the more experienced heads in the team. Burton had also been knocked out of the FA Cup when they travelled to Cheshire on a dark, dank afternoon in December for an FA Trophy first-round tie at Northwich Victoria. The few hardy Burton fans among the 670 at the Drill Field could not have imagined that a welcome 2-0 victory over the Conference club would be the first step on the road to Wembley.

However, Burton began to haul themselves away from the Northern Premier League relegation zone and in the FA Trophy second round they swept Conference side Weymouth aside 3-0 at Eton Park. But it was not until Whitley Bay were disposed of in the next round that trophy fever really hit town.

The quarter-finals drew Burton with Maidstone United, at that time a leading non-League force and one of the favourites to make it to Wembley. A Paul Groves goal in Kent brought Maidstone back to Burton for a reply and a Dave Redfern goal saw off the Stones in front of a 3,316-strong crowd.

The semi-final pitched Albion against another Kent team and former finalists, Dartford. Although Dartford had been relegated the previous season, they were now flying under the management of Peter Taylor. An attendance of 3,690 saw Burton come from behind to win the home leg 2-1 with goals from Paul Groves and Bob Gauden, but that looked a narrow margin to defend in Kent. However, roared on by over 1,000 travelling fans, Burton stunned Dartford with a Paul Bancroft goal after just two minutes. Dartford never recovered and Bancroft added a second just before half-time to effectively kill the tie before the interval. Burton were on their way to Wembley.

Routes to the Final

Kidderminster Harriers

First round	Kidderminster Harriers 0, Mossley 0
First-round replay	Mossley 0, Kidderminster Harriers 1
Second round	Kidderminster Harriers 2, Worthing 0
Third round	Kidderminster Harriers 3, Cheltenham Town 2
Fourth round	Dagenham 0, Kidderminster Harriers 3
Semi-final, first leg	Kidderminster Harriers 0, Fareham Town 0
Semi-final, second leg	Fareham Town 0, Kidderminster Harriers 2

Burton Albion

First round	Northwich Victoria 0, Burton Albion 2
Second round	Burton Albion 3, Weymouth 0
Third round	Burton Albion 1, Whitley Bay 0
Fourth round	Maidstone United 1, Burton Albion 1
Fourth-round replay	Burton Albion 1, Maidstone United 0
Semi-final, first leg	Burton Albion 2, Dartford 1
Semi-final, second leg	Dartford 0, Burton Albion 2

1988

Enfield 0, Telford United 0
Wembley, 7 May 1988

The champagne stayed on ice as Enfield and Telford went through the odd experience of a Wembley final without goals, victors or losers. While 120 minutes of stalemate did nothing to spoil the occasion for either club or their fans, the after-match 'celebrations' had a strange feel to them as the teams looked ahead to a replay at The Hawthorns the following Thursday. The players trooped up the stairs to the Royal Box, shook hands with guest of honour Gordon Banks, and came down again for a friendly photo session on the pitch. But, with no trophy or medals to show off, there was an unavoidable feeling of emptiness. Telford goalkeeper Kevin Charlton summed up the atmosphere. 'You don't feel elation, you don't feel disappointment – nothing', he said. 'You just have to say "we've had a nice weekend, now we'll play them again on Thursday."'

The match itself fluctuated between long periods of disappointing inactivity and short bursts of goalmouth incident. Enfield took the first-half honours and missed a couple of inviting second-half chances, before Telford staged a late onslaught that threatened to end the game there and then. Telford carried that momentum into extra time and almost produced a dramatic conclusion seconds before the end of the extra half hour. Steve Norris controlled a Harry Wiggins pass to gain an extra second in the danger area. He used that to turn the ball to substitute Tony Griffiths, who steamed in and shot, only to see the ball blocked on its goal-wards path.

Griffiths, in fact, played more than a ninety-minute game after Telford forward John Stringer broke down only twenty-eight minutes after his return from a niggling hamstring injury. Both sides were still showing signs of nerves at that stage and it was Enfield who nearly took advantage. Confusion reigned at Enfield's first corner and Iain Sankey had to clear Nigel Keen's shot with Charlton beaten. Telford's best spell came soon afterwards, when Steve Nelson had two close-range headers blocked.

From then until the interval, however, Enfield looked the more composed and brought an excellent double save out of Charlton from Paul Harding and Robin Lewis. After the interval, Telford's Man of the Match Paul Mayman finally got some life out of their midfield and Iain Sankey nearly struck on sixty minutes. Some sections of the crowd thought his twenty-five-yard shot had gone in, but it had hit the stanchion on the wrong side of the net. Robin Lewis missed with two headers for Enfield, but Telford had upped the tempo and suddenly Enfield 'keeper Andy Pape was a busy man. He palmed away a well-struck free-kick from Wiggins in extra time and then Steve Biggins was denied by a timely and crucial tackle from the impressive Brian Cottington.

Then it was time to look forward to The Hawthorns, where less salubrious surroundings on a Thursday night were in fact to provide for a much more exciting final second time around.

Telford United: Charlton, McGinty, Wiggins, Mayman, Nelson, Storton, Joseph, Biggins, Norris, Sankey, Stringer. Substitutes: Griffiths, Hancock.

Enfield: Pape, Cooper, Sparrow, Howell, Keen, Francis, Lewis, Cottington, Furlong, Harding, King. Substitutes: Edmonds, Hayzelden.

Enfield 3, Telford United 2
The Hawthorns, 12 May 1988

Enfield lifted the FA Trophy for the second time after a replay that was in stark contrast to the previous Saturday's game at Wembley. Just fewer than 7,000 spectators witnessed a pulsating game in which fortunes fluctuated wildly, with Enfield getting the better of five goals of varying quality, plus almost every other incident imaginable around the goals guarded by Andy Pape and Kevin Charlton. Indeed, had it not been for two outstanding performances from both 'keepers, The Hawthorns could have been engulfed by a goal glut.

Telford bettered Enfield for the first twenty-five minutes, before the Londoners composed themselves and took control with some tidy football, thanks to the ceaseless influence of Paul Harding. But Telford found new life again to take the tie to the brink of extra time, only to be sunk nine minutes from the end. It was Harding who swept past John McGinty and found Steve King, who knocked the ball across the goal for Robin Lewis to lunge at and Paul Furlong to bundle the ball over the line. It was an outcome that had looked most unlikely on thirteen minutes, when Telford took the lead in front of around 6,000 of their fans in the crowd of 6,919.

Substitute Mark Cunningham, who came on after just eleven minutes following an ankle injury to Paul Mayman, provided a cross for Steve Biggins to tap in from five yards. But the game twisted back to Enfield before half-time. On twenty-three minutes, David Howell planted a glancing header past Charlton from a Nigel Keen free-kick. Then, just before the interval whistle, Enfield were ahead in bizarre circumstances when Furlong attempted a cross that looped over everyone and into the net.

Telford picked themselves up again and were within a whisker of an equaliser on seventy-five minutes, when Cunningham hit the inside of the post and the ball was hoofed away for a corner. Enfield were shaken, and almost immediately Telford were level. Nick Francis was adjudged to have handled Iain Sankey's corner and Steve Norris converted the penalty. With the crowd behind them, Telford looked set to go in for the kill, with Brian Sparrow somehow clearing a Steve Nelson header on the line. But they had reckoned without Enfield's never-say-die spirit that saw Furlong have the final say. Delighted Enfield manager Eddie McCluskey said, 'It was great for the game and there was a good feeling between the players. Both games were played in a tremendous spirit.' The winners' lap of honour ended in mutual applause and even many handshakes between Enfield supporters and a hundred or so Telford fans, who stayed behind to provide a heart-warming reminder of the non-League spirit. It could hardly have been a better night for the game as a whole.

Telford United: Charlton, McGinty, Wiggins, Mayman, Nelson, Storton, Joseph, Biggins, Norris, Sankey, Griffiths. Substitutes: Cunningham, Hancock.

Enfield: Pape, Cooper, Sparrow, Howell, Keen, Francis, Lewis, Cottington, Furlong, Harding, King. Substitutes: Edmonds, Scott.

In Focus
Enfield's True Reward

No one could deny Enfield's right to lift the FA Trophy after coming through 6 matches from the semi-final stage. The Londoners made smooth progress through the early rounds of the competition, with a notable scalp in the fourth round when they beat Lincoln City – who would go on to win promotion back into the Football League – 1-0. But they then overcame a mighty tussle with Barrow, plus the 210 minutes against Telford, to finally claim their prize.

Enfield were drawn away for the first leg of the semi-final and made the long journey to Barrow knowing they would face a noisy, partisan crowd of over 6,000. Perhaps the home fans put too much pressure on the home team, as Enfield settled well and took the lead on twenty-seven minutes. A rare error from Barrow goalkeeper Jeff Wealands saw him fail to collect Nigel Keen's free-kick and Nicky Francis headed into an empty net. But Barrow equalised in dramatic style just before half-time, when Micky Carroll unleashed a thirty-five-yard shot that flew past Andy Paper – a goal considered by many Barrow supporters as one of the best ever seen at Holker Street.

Barrow took control in the second half but, after missing several good chances, were stunned in injury time when Andy Edmonds' cross to the near post was headed past Wealands by Francis. If Enfield thought that they had done the hard work they got a rude awakening just thirty seconds into the second leg. As Enfield's players passed the ball around after the kick-off, Dave Howell was caught in possession on the edge of the box by Danny Wheatley, who steered the ball past the helpless Pape. Enfield never fully recovered, and, although Francis hit the post with a header, the sides were deadlocked and had to go a neutral venue at Kidderminster to settle the issue – or so people expected.

Barrow looked the likely winners at Kidderminster and it was no surprise when in the fifty-seventh minute Wheatley ran onto a through ball to beat Pape. But, as ever, Enfield never knew when they were beaten and somehow they managed to swing the game around. With twelve minutes remaining, teenager Paul Furlong came on for Martin Duffield and with his first touch his shot caught Kenny Gordon and looped over Wealands. Steve King almost won the game for Enfield towards the end of extra time, but both clubs had to move on to another replay at Stafford.

By now there was little that either side did not know about each other and it was no surprise that scoring chances were few and far between. Twelve minutes into the second half, Enfield midfielder Robin Lewis, who turned in a match-winning performance, made ground on the right and his cross found the unmarked King, who gratefully drove the ball past Wealands. In injury time, Barrow forced a series of corners, but the Enfield defence, in which Howell was outstanding, managed to hold them at bay.

Routes to the Final

Enfield

First round	Enfield 4, Worthing 2
Second round	Enfield 3 Bishops Stortford 1
Third round	Witton Albion 1, Enfield 2
Fourth round	Enfield 1, Lincoln City 0
Semi-final, first leg	Barrow 1, Enfield 2
Semi-final, second leg	Enfield 0, Barrow 1
Semi-final, first replay (at Kidderminster)	Enfield 1, Barrow 1
Semi-final, second replay (at Stafford)	Enfield 1, Barrow 0

THE FOOTBALL ASSOCIATION

CHALLENGE TROPHY FINAL

ANNIVERSARY

SATURDAY 7 MAY 1988
Kick-off 3.00 p.m.

Enfield v Telford United

 WEMBLEY
—— WHERE ELSE ——

Official Programme £1.00

Programme for the 1988 FA Trophy final between Enfield and Telford United.

Telford United

First round	Buxton 2, Telford United 4
Second round	Wealdstone 0, Telford United 2
Third round	Telford United 1, Stafford Rangers 1
Third-round replay	Stafford Rangers 2, Telford United 3
Fourth round	Cheltenham Town 2, Telford United 4
Semi-final, first leg	Telford United 2, Wokingham Town 0
Semi-final, second leg	Wokingham Town 0, Telford United 2

1989

Telford United 1, Macclesfield Town 0
Wembley, 13 May 1989

Super-sub Ian Crawley was Telford's hero as his side took the FA Trophy for the third time, following a gruelling two-hour battle against Macclesfield. Crawley, who scored VS Rugby's winner in the 1983 FA Vase final, was disappointed to be left out of the starting eleven but ended up singing the evening away with delight after his ninety-fifth-minute winner. The striker, who later that evening was to give a cabaret turn and even DJ at the club's banquet, was on hand when Macclesfield goalkeeper Alan Zelem misjudged a ball pumped into the area by Telford captain Andy Lee. Letting the ball bounce, Zelem saw it zip off the lush Wembley turf and over his head for Crawley, who pounced to simply dispatch the ball into an empty net.

It was cruel on Zelem, who had not put a foot wrong all afternoon, and on Macclesfield, who continued to fight all the way to the end of extra time. In fact, the final thirty minutes proved to be the most exciting of the game. Gaps began to appear where none had been previously and more goalmouth action than in the previous ninety minutes kept the crowd on their toes until the end.

Kevin Charlton made a diving save from Steve Burr to maintain Telford's advantage and Zelem made up for his earlier mishap by turning a Tony Griffiths scorcher round for a corner. The Silkmen made one last push when Burr's left footer was deflected for a corner that was cleared and Telford had avenged the defeat in 1970 in the first ever trophy final.

Earlier, the ninety minutes of normal time had perhaps seen Macclesfield have the edge, but Telford's disciplined defence limited the Silkmen's chances. Central defender Mark Hancock, recalled to the Telford side because of an injury to Trevor Storton, was calm and composed in tandem with young Chris Brindley, who belied his nineteen years with a kingpin performance. It was in attack that Telford lacked many ideas, and forwards Tommy Lloyd and John Stringer fought a frustrating and unrewarding battle to find something out of the crumbs that came their way. A first-half header from defender Steve Nelson was the nearest that Telford came to scoring.

Charlton came to Telford's rescue in the thirty-fourth minute when he tipped over a flashing header from Graham Tobin, but although Burr and John Timmons were often a problem Macclesfield also failed to find what was really needed to break the deadlock. All in all, it seemed a somewhat quiet final in front of a crowd of 18,106, with Macclesfield ending the day feeling a little hard done by.

But, as Telford manager Stan Storton delightedly embraced all thirteen of his players in the middle of the Wembley pitch, a saying that used to be displayed in the Telford boardroom came to mind. It read: 'Those who win can laugh. Others can please themselves.'

Telford United: Charlton, Lee, Wiggins, Mayman, Brindley, Hancock, Joseph, Grainger, Lloyd, Stringer, Nelson. Substitutes: Crawley, Griffiths.

Macclesfield Town: Zelem, Roberts, Hardman, Edwards, Tobin, Hanlon, Askey, Timmons, Lake, Burr, Imrie. Substitutes: Derbyshire, Kendall.

In Focus
Five Finals for Telford

As 1970 finalists, Telford were quick to make their mark on the FA Trophy and they became one of the competition's dominant forces up to and including 1989. Victory in 1971 was followed by reaching the semi-finals the following year and, though several lean years followed, Telford were back at Wembley, and lifting the trophy, in 1983. Five years on an epic tussle with Enfield ended in defeat, but, just as they had done in 1971, Telford returned with a vengeance the following year. Their three wins remains a record held jointly with Scarborough and Woking, but they have appeared in more finals – five – than any other club.

Telford United's FA Trophy record, 1969-1989:

1969/70

Third qualifying round	Telford United 5, Witton Albion 0
First round	Ilkeston Town 0, Telford United 2
Second round	Telford United 1, Wigan Athletic 0
Third round	Romford 1, Telford United 1
Third-round replay	Telford United 2, Romford 1
Fourth round	Worcester City 1, Telford United 3
Semi-final (at Swindon)	Telford United 2, Chelmsford City 0
Final (at Wembley)	Macclesfield Town 2, Telford United 0

1970/71

First round	Telford United 6, Bradford Park Avenue 1
Second round	Telford United 7, South Shields 1
Third round	Burton Albion 0, Telford United 2
Fourth round	Tamworth 1, Telford United 1
Fourth-round replay	Telford United 6, Tamworth 1
Semi-final (at West Bromwich)	Telford United 3, Yeovil 1
Final (at Wembley)	Telford United 3, Hillingdon Borough 2

1971/72

First round	Nuneaton Borough 1, Telford United 2
Second round	South Liverpool 2, Telford United 3
Third round	Dorchester Town 1, Telford United 1
Third-round replay	Telford United 3, Dorchester Town 1
Fourth round	Buxton 2, Telford United 2
Fourth-round replay	Telford United 2, Buxton 1
Semi-final (at Northampton)	Barnet 1, Telford United 0

1972/73

First round	Telford United 1, Altrincham 1
First-round replay	Altrincham 2, Telford United 0

1973/74

First round	Telford United 5, Chorley 1
Second round	Boston United 2, Telford United 1

1974/75

First round	Stourbridge 2, Telford United 2
First-round replay	Telford United 4, Stourbridge 0
Second round	Morecambe 2, Telford United 3
Third round	Wimbledon 4, Telford United 1

1975/76

First round	Bangor City 1, Telford United 2
Second round	Atherstone Town 1, Telford United 1
Second-round replay	Telford United 1, Atherstone Town 2

1976/77

First round	Telford United 1, Stafford Rangers 1
First-round replay	Stafford Rangers 1, Telford United 0

Above: Telford's players and management in jubilant mood after their 1-0 victory over Macclesfield Town.

Left: Telford manager Stan Storton holds the FA Trophy high.

1977/78
Third qualifying round   Hednesford Town 4, Telford United 2

1978/79
Third qualifying round   Eastwood Town 1, Telford United 0

1979/80
First round   Bangor City 5, Telford United 1

1980/81
Third qualifying round   Bedworth United 1, Telford United 0

1981/82
First qualifying round   Telford United 1, Moor Green 1
First qualifying-round replay   Moor Green 0, Telford United 2
Second qualifying round   Bilston 1, Telford United 2
Third qualifying round   Telford United 5, Nantwich Town 0
First round   Telford United 1, Burton Albion 0
Second round   Telford United 0, Bedford Town 0
Second-round replay   Bedford Town 0, Telford United 3
Third round   Telford United 0, Enfield 1

1982/83
First round   Burton Albion 0, Telford United 1
Second round   Spennymoor United 0, Telford United 0
Second-round replay   Telford United 2, Spennymoor United 1
Third round   Telford United 3, Scarborough 0
Fourth round   Telford United 4, Dartford 0
Semi-final, first leg   Telford United 0, Harrow Borough 2
Semi-final, second leg   Harrow Borough 1, Telford United 5
Final (at Wembley)   Telford United 2, Northwich Victoria 1

1983/84
First round   Mossley 1, Telford United 2
Second round   Telford United 2, Runcorn 1
Third round   Telford United 2, Bromsgrove Rovers 0
Fourth round   Telford United 3, Marine 3
Fourth-round replay   Marine 2, Telford United 0

1984/85
First round   Northwich Victoria 0, Telford United 4
Second round   Telford United 1, Fisher Athletic 2

1985/86
First round   Telford United 2, Southport 4

1986/87
First round   Telford United 1, Nuneaton Borough 4

1987/88
First round   Buxton 2, Telford United 4
Second round   Wealdstone 0, Telford United 2
Third round   Telford United 1, Stafford Rangers 1
Third-round replay   Stafford Rangers 2, Telford United 3
Fourth round   Cheltenham Town 2, Telford United 4
Semi-final, first leg   Telford United 2, Wokingham Town 0
Semi-final, second leg   Wokingham Town 0, Telford United 2
Final (at Wembley)   Telford United 0, Enfield 0
Final replay
(at West Bromwich Albion)   Enfield 3, Telford United 2

1988/89
First round   Telford United 3, Witton Albion 0
Second round   Yeovil Town 1, Telford United 4
Third round   Kidderminster Harriers 1, Telford United 1
Third-round replay   Telford United 2, Kidderminster Harriers 0
Fourth round   Newcastle Blue Star 1, Telford United 4
Semi-final, first leg   Hyde United 0, Telford United 1
Semi-final, second leg   Telford United 3, Hyde United 0
Final (at Wembley)   Telford United 1, Macclesfield Town 0

Routes to the Final

Telford United
First round   Telford United 3, Witton Albion 0
Second round   Yeovil Town 1, Telford United 4
Third round   Kidderminster Harriers 1, Telford United 1
Third-round replay   Telford United 2, Kidderminster Harriers 0
Fourth round   Newcastle Blue Star 1, Telford United 4
Semi-final, first leg   Hyde United 0, Telford United 1
Semi-final, second leg   Telford United 3, Hyde United 0

Macclesfield Town
First round   Marine 2, Macclesfield Town 2
First-round replay   Macclesfield Town 4, Marine 1
Second round   South Bank 0, Macclesfield Town 3
Third round   Macclesfield Town 2, Gravesend & Northfleet 0
Fourth round   Macclesfield Town 1, Welling United 0
Semi-final, first leg   Dartford 0, Macclesfield Town 0
Semi-final, second leg   Macclesfield Town 4, Dartford 1

1990

Barrow 3, Leek Town 0
Wembley, 19 May 1990

Fans' favourites Kenny Gordon and Colin Cowperthwaite were the heroes for Barrow as the club swept away the memories of eighteen difficult non-League years with a day to remember at Wembley. The former Football League side beatplucky Leek with goals from two of their most loyal servants. Local-born Gordon, playing his final game before emigrating to Australia, joined Barrow in 1978 and stayed, bar one season with Morecambe. Cowperthwaite arrived in 1977 and stayed to notch 704 appearances and 282 goals.

It was a day of tearful emotions of joy for Barrow, who rose to the occasion and left Leek with nothing to offer save honest endeavour. Leek had only one weak shot in the first half, as Barrow quickly asserted themselves, with midfielders Kenny Lowe, Peter Farrell and Kevin Proctor laying the foundations for flowing football. Leek abandoned thoughts of a counter-attack and, with wingers Neil Doherty and Paul Ferris causing a host of problems, it really was a question of when rather than whether Barrow would score. Barrow's opener was timed to perfection – just before the interval. Right-back Steve Higgins sent over a looping cross straight into Gordon's path and his glancing header flashed past Leek 'keeper Robin Simpson and into the net.

At the start of the second half Northern Premier League Leek finally showed why they had dispatched Conference opposition and won so many admirers in reaching the final from the qualifying stages. Four successive corners put Barrow on the back foot and it took an amazing save from Peter McDonnell to prevent Leek getting right back into the match. A floating cross was met firmly by the head of Leek striker Dave Sutton, but McDonnell leapt to somehow scoop the ball to safety. It was cruel for Leek and moments later they were buried by two quick Barrow knockout punches. First Farrell hit a perfect centre to Ferris, who flicked on for Cowperthwaite to head home confidently.

Above left: Barrow fans' favourite Colin Cowperthwaite keeps a tight hold on the FA Trophy.

Above right: The whole of Barrow seems to have turned out for the team's triumphant homecoming.

Right: Kenny Gordon flies in for Barrow's second goal.

Moments later the contest was over, as Gordon converted another precision cross, this time from Lowe, which left Leek flat-footed. The celebrations could begin. Special mention for Barrow must go to manager Ray Wilkie, who took over Barrow as a struggling Northern Premier League side in 1986 and took them into the Conference. He captured the hearts of not just the club but also the community, as a quarter of the town's population travelled to Wembley to savour an unforgettable day. Emlyn Hughes OBE, who was born in Barrow-in-Furness and began his illustrious career with Barrow's youth side, said, 'Ray came to Barrow when the town was dead and buried as far as football was concerned for the last twenty years. He picked them up, resurrected them, and he did it by picking players who wanted to play for a club called Barrow AFC.' Wilkie admitted, 'It was like a "Roy of the Rovers" story for me. It was the best performance I ever saw Barrow give; whether it was the right time or the right place or whether someone up there loves me, loves the players, loves Barrow, I don't know.'

Barrow: McDonnell, Higgins, Skivington, Gordon, Chilton, Farrell, Lowe, Proctor, Doherty, Cowperthwaite, Ferris. Substitutes: Burgess, Gilmour.

Leek: Simpson, Elsby, Pearce, McMullen, Clowes, Coleman, Mellor, Somerville, Sutton, Millington, Norris. Substitutes: Smith, Russell.

In Focus
Barrow Come in from the Cold

Barrow rank, in my view, as the most romantic winners of the FA Trophy. Here was a club that had been cast from the Football League into the wilderness, only to bounce back nearly eighteen years later with a victory on English football's greatest stage. With the lines between Conference and Division Three increasingly blurred these days, it is hard to comprehend what a hammer blow it was to lose one's Football League status in the days of re-election. Effectively, there was no way back.

2 June 1972 became known as 'Black Friday' for supporters of Barrow AFC. Sure, Barrow had endured a tough season in Division Four, but had finished third bottom, 8 points clear of Crewe. Another couple of points would have seen them in the comfort zone. While the re-election process would be nail-biting, there was no cause for undue alarm. But, on an extraordinary second vote, following a 26-26 tie, Hereford were voted in by twenty-nine votes to Barrow's twenty.

Ron Duxbury recalls:

When Barrow reached the FA Trophy final in 1990, I produced a documentary about the history of Barrow, and of course 'Black Friday' came into it. I interviewed the then president, Sam Morgan. He told me that he had gone to the meeting with life member, Dennis Rose. He said that he (Sam) was sat next to Jack Charlton, who just sat with his mouth open, not believing that Barrow had been voted out. He said it was then a matter of going 'cap in hand' to whichever league would take Barrow, and it was the Northern Premier League. He said that those early days were bleak, as the player registrations belonged to the Football League. Barrow were not allowed to pay players, and those early non-League days were a real struggle. In the same programme I spoke to Neil McDonald, who said he literally cried into his beer in the Sandgate.

For Barrow FC's website editor Jim Whitton, it is a day etched in his memory.

On the fateful day in 1972, I was in my small bedsit in Preston, where I was the working at the time. I had actually forgotten that there was a vote that day (this perhaps says something for our confidence or complacency). The radio was on and I was only half listening to the sports news: 'Cup giant-killers Hereford United have been admitted to the Football League…' It didn't register, at least for a second or two, until I caught the word 'Barrow' and realised that we had been voted out. Gutted is an overused word these days, but that's how it felt, almost literally. A sick feeling in the pit of the stomach.

Disbelief and despair turned to anger, us? Hereford had done nothing in their League, just had a bit of luck in the cup. It just seemed like the end of the world. You wanted to do something about it, but realised there was no hope.

John Dale recalls:

I'd been for a job interview 120 miles from Barrow, was driving back, and heard the news on the radio about 4.30 p.m. I was so mortified, I had to pull in at the next service station for an hour and let it sink in. I never thought it would be us. We weren't bottom after all, I'd been to all the last few home games, we were playing well, it was only because all the 'keepers on the books were injured and we weren't allowed sign anyone else, as the transfer deadline had passed, we therefore had to play outfield players in goal. 3 or 4 games to go we were out of the re-election area, everything looked to be ok. We then lost the last few games because we didn't have a 'keeper. One win (2 points in those days) would have seen us out the bottom four. We know the rest. Stockport and Crewe were below us, and look where they are now!

Routes to the Final

Barrow

First round	Barrow 1, Bangor City 0
Second round	Barrow 1, Metropolitan Police 0
Third round	Yeovil Town 1, Barrow 1
Third-round replay	Barrow 2, Yeovil Town 1
Fourth round	Kingstonian 2, Barrow 2
Fourth-round replay	Barrow 1, Kingstonian 0
Semi-final, first leg	Colne Dynamoes 0, Barrow 1
Semi-final, second leg	Barrow 1, Colne Dynamoes 0

Leek Town

First qualifying round	Leek Town 3, Hednesford Town 1
Second qualifying round	Moor Green 1, Leek Town 3
Third qualifying round	Newtown 0, Leek Town 1
First round	Spennymoor United 1, Leek Town 2
Second round	Leek Town 1, Nuneaton Borough 1
Second-round replay	Nuneaton Borough 0, Leek Town 1
Third round	Telford United 0, Leek Town 0
Third-round replay	Leek Town 3, Telford United 0
Fourth round	Leek Town 1, Darlington 0
Semi-final, first leg	Stafford Rangers 0, Leek Town 0
Semi-final, second leg	Leek Town 1, Stafford Rangers 0

1991

Wycombe Wanderers 2, Kidderminster Harriers 1
Wembley, 11 May 1991

Mark West perfectly capped a fine season for Wycombe Wanderers with a brilliant winning goal to capture the FA Trophy for non-League's fastest emerging side. Wycombe, riding high in the Conference under the management of Martin O'Neill, and ensconced in their brand new Adams Park stadium, won the cup in front of a record crowd of 34,842, with 25,000 of them supporting Wycombe. Wycombe deserved to win as they played with more verve, tackled more directly and defended more tightly. But Kidderminster, who played some neat football in the middle of the park, created a good slice of chances. However, a failure to convert any of three first-half openings left Wycombe in the driving seat.

It was Wycombe who drew first blood after a tentative opening fifteen minutes. On sixteen minutes, in only the game's second chance, Steve Guppy put West away down the left wing as Kidderminster's defence left him onside and Keith Scott was on hand at the post to force the ball home. The goal shook Kidderminster into action. On twenty-six minutes, Steve Lilwall burst between two Wycombe players into the penalty area. He chose to shoot early, from the corner of the box, and Blues 'keeper John Granville saved comfortably.

Lilwall continued to be the star attraction for Kidderminster, setting up captain Antone Joseph to shoot wide when unmarked and then feeding Dave Hadley to cross for Delwyn Humphreys, who headed over. But Wycombe, content to hit Kidderminster on the break while they held a goal advantage, always looked sharp and dangerous. On twenty-eight minutes Guppy and Stuart Cash combined to set up Scott, who played a one-two with West before unleashing a left-footer that Kidderminster goalkeeper Paul Jones touched round the post. Three minutes later, West embarked on a surging run only to be brought down by David Barnett, just outside the penalty area. Barnett could have no complaints as he went in the referee's notebook.

Wycombe definitely had the greater presence and as the second half ticked along it looked as if they were set to coast to a fairly comfortable, if narrow, margin victory. But on sixty minutes Kidderminster created a goal out of the blue. Full-back John McGrath volleyed a delicate ball forward to Hadley, who reached the edge of the area and shot low but without power. But Granville let the ball slip under his body and Kidderminster were level.

If Kidderminster saw hope, the goal only served to ignite Wycombe to take control. Just four minutes later, centre half Glyn Creaser played a ball down the right wing to Scott. The winger played an early cross as West sprinted into the area. The centre was knee-high but West continued his momentum to time a diving header to perfection and the ball shot past Jones. It was an instinctive striker's goal and one that deserved to go down as a Wembley winner.

Granville redeemed himself in the closing minutes with some assertive keeping to hold Kidderminster at bay, notably saving well from the still lively Lilwall. Then the nail-biting was over and Wycombe had won at Wembley in their first appearance there since winning the FA Amateur Cup final back in 1957.

Wycombe Wanderers: Granville, Crossley, Cash, Kerr, Creaser, Carroll, Ryan, Stapleton, West, Scott, Guppy. Substitutes: Hutchinson, Robinson.

Kidderminster Harriers: Jones, Kurila, McGrath, Weir, Barnett, Forsyth, Joseph, Howell, Hadley, Lilwall, Humphreys. Substitutes: Wilcox, Whitehouse.

In Focus
Changing Face of the Trophy Programme

By 1991, the official FA Trophy match programme had adapted the magazine style format that has become synonymous with major cup finals and internationals. The modern style generally does not go down that well with collectors, who tend to prefer the traditional size programmes that are much easier to store and far less expensive to post. The programme for 1991 was forty-four pages in length, but its only real claim to superiority over the earliest issues was just slightly more reading matter and colour photographs. Nineteen of the pages – almost half – were wholly advertisements, which says something about the way the game had become highly commercial by 1991, though the cover price of £2 was not too extravagant. By 1999, an almost identical style of issue had shot up in price to £3.50.

The first final programme of 1970, which retailed at two shillings, was certainly just as adequate as the 1991 issue, despite being of the traditional programme size and just sixteen pages in length. Player and club profiles were included, plus a photograph from Macclesfield's semi-final tie against Barnet, and only four full pages were devoted to advertising. In 1972 a green cover with a photograph of the trophy was adopted, and this style remained constant up to and including 1977, with the content and layout pretty much the same as it had been from the outset. Variations on the

Above: Wycombe's players parade the FA Trophy to their fans.

Right: Celebrations begin for Wycombe after their 2-1 victory over Kidderminster Harriers.

Below: The Wycombe side takes to the field before the final.

theme of a cover depicting the cup were used through to 1985, with a slight increase in size and an upping of the number of pages, by 1985, to twenty-four. The year 1984 saw the need to produce a replay programme, at very short notice, for the first time after the draw between Bangor City and Northwich Victoria. A very basic issue was put together for the replay at Stoke, though it did include photographs from the Wembley game.

It was in 1986 that the brochure style of programme emerged for the first time, though oddly this was dropped for 1987 and 1988. In 1987 another drawn final saw a replay just three days later at West Bromwich and a very good job was done in producing an issue, including new articles plus photographs from the previous Saturday's meeting between Burton Albion and Kidderminster Harriers. It was in 1989 that the larger brochure-type programme was re-adopted and that format, with steady expansion of the number of pages, has held sway ever since.

Routes to the Final

Wycombe Wanderers

First round	Wycombe Wanderers 1, Wealdstone 0
Second round	VS Rugby 0, Wycombe Wanderers 1
Third round	Wycombe Wanderers 2, Cheltenham Town 1
Fourth round	Northwich Victoria 2, Wycombe Wanderers 3
Semi-final, first leg	Wycombe Wanderers 2, Altrincham 1
Semi-final, second leg	Altrincham 0, Wycombe Wanderers 2

Kidderminster Harriers

First round	Kidderminster Harriers 4, Sutton United 2
Second round	Kidderminster Harriers 1, Dover Athletic 0
Third round	Kidderminster Harriers 3, Bath City 1
Fourth round	Kidderminster Harriers 3, Emley 0
Semi-final, first leg	Kidderminster Harriers 1, Witton Albion 0
Semi-final, second leg	Witton Albion 4, Kidderminster Harriers 3
Semi-final replay (at Stafford Rangers)	Kidderminster Harriers 2, Witton Albion 1

1992

Colchester United 3, Witton Albion 1
Wembley, 10 May 1992

Conference Champions Colchester United proved too strong for Witton Albion in a final that went according to the script. Colchester, who stormed back into the Football League in the same season following an epic tussle with Wycombe Wanderers, were simply too strong for the Witton side, but at least Witton went down playing attacking football. The only blot on the day was that it was an unusually bad-tempered affair, with four bookings for Witton, two for Colchester, plus the sending off of U's Jason Cook by referee Keren Barrett.

Around eighty per cent of the 27,806 crowd were backing the U's and they were celebrating after just five minutes. Vastly experienced defender Paul Roberts launched a trademark long throw into the area that player-manager Roy McDonough flicked on to Mike Masters, and the American forward sneaked in front of Witton 'keeper Keith Mason to put his side ahead. In so doing, Masters achieved his personal ambition to become the first American to score a goal at Wembley.

Witton were undaunted by their early setback and prolific striker Karl Thomas probed the U's defence. But after Colchester banged in a splendid second on twenty minutes, the Cheshire side were left chasing the game. Cook initiated the move with a telling pass that sent teenage starlet Mark Kinsella clear of the defence. The Republic of Ireland youth international put in a well-timed centre that was just too far in front of Steve McGavin's outstretched toe, but Nicky Smith was charging in down the left and hit the net from twelve yards out.

Witton became more rugged and soon Jim Connor, Lee Coathup and Andy Grimshaw were booked – but they also showed that they could produce flowing football without the need to recourse to the physical side. Former Crewe midfielder Colin Rose gave the U's defence plenty to think about and forced the save of the match from Scott Barrett on thirty-five minutes. He beat the defence and shot well with the goal at his mercy, but Barrett managed to deflect his low shot wide of the post.

The corner that followed caused more problems for Colchester, but Cook cleared from under the bar as Thomas attempted to net a cross fumbled by Barrett. Colchester really should have sealed the match before half-time, Kinsella weaving through the Witton defence but then somehow shooting wide from ten yards. Witton sensed a lifeline and they briefly got back into the game on fifty-seven minutes. Coathup put in a cross and Mike Lutkevitch showed his eye for the goal by beating Tony English to send a header looping out of Barrett's reach. That, however, proved to be the extent of Witton's fightback and Colchester should have quickly wrapped matters up. Masters hit the outside of the post and substitute Gary Bennett had a shot deflected for a corner.

But on eighty-two minutes the day was partly spoiled for the U's and particularly Cook. He was manhandled by Jim McCluskie as he tried to keep possession and lashed out with a punch. Given a case of clear violent conduct, the only option was a straight red. That might have spelt disaster for Colchester, but it simply served to buoy them for the closing minutes. They never looked in danger, and in the third minute of stoppage time, with Witton leaving gaps in a tired search for a goal, Masters set up McGavin to run clear and score unhindered from fifteen yards.

Colchester United: Barrett, Donald, Roberts, Kinsella, English, Martin, Cook, Masters, McDonough, McGavin, Smith. Substitutes: Bennett, Collins.

Witton Albion: Mason, Halliday, Coathup, McNeilis, Jim Connor, Anderson, Thomas, Rose, Alford, Grimshaw, Lutkevitch. Substitutes: Joe Connor, McCluskie.

In Focus
First FA Sponsor Gave Trophy Boost

The Football Association agreed terms for the first ever sponsorship for a senior FA competition when Vauxhall Motors became the inaugural sponsors of the FA Trophy for 1991/92. The motor car manufacturer agreed to lend its support for one season, with £30,000 in prize money being made available. Winners Colchester United scooped £6,000, with £4,000 going to Witton Albion. Losing semi-finalists Marine and Barrow took £1,500 each, while the losing quarter-finalist was awarded £750. Those clubs that reached the third round earned £400 each, with £200 for those that only made it to the second round. Unibond League side Marine also won £1,000 for progressing furthest in the competition as a club non-exempt from entry at the first-round stage. The Crosby-based club certainly earned their prize by playing no less than 12 matches from the first qualifying round – where they needed two replays to overcome Nuneaton Borough – to the semi-finals, where they were beaten by Witton over two legs.

Southport took £500 for the largest away win, a 5-0 victory at Alnwick Town in the first qualifying round, and also shared £750 for the largest winning margin with

Right: Colchester's FA Trophy success capped an extraordinary season in which they also won the Nationwide Conference title and promotion back to the Football League.

Below: Colchester celebrations.

Farnborough Town who, in an ironic twist, beat Southport 5-0 in the second round proper!

Southport were again among the money for all victories by a three-goal margin or more, not only for the win over Alnwick but also for beating North Shields 4-1 and Rhyl 3-0 in the qualifying stages. However, they had to take a share of £3,000 with thirty-one other clubs!

Routes to the Final

Colchester United

First round	Colchester United 2, Kingstonian 2
First-round replay	Kingstonian 2, Colchester United 3
Second round	Merthyr Tydfil 0, Colchester United 0
Second-round replay	Colchester United 1, Merthyr Tydfil 0
Third round	Colchester United 3, Morecambe 1
Fourth round	Colchester United 4, Telford United 0
Semi-final, first leg	Colchester United 3, Macclesfield Town 0
Semi-final, second leg	Macclesfield Town 1, Colchester United 1

Witton Albion

First round	Witton Albion 2, Billingham Synthonia 2
First-round replay	Billingham Synthonia 1, Witton Albion 2
Second round	Witton Albion 1, Aylesbury United 0
Third round	Witton Albion 1, Stalybridge Celtic 0
Fourth round	Wycombe Wanderers 1, Witton Albion 2
Semi-final first leg	Witton Albion 2, Marine 2
Semi-final second leg	Marine 1, Witton Albion 4

1993

Wycombe Wanderers 4, Runcorn 1
Wembley, 9 May 1993

Wycombe Wanderers added the FA Trophy to the GM Vauxhall Conference by sweeping aside Runcorn at Wembley in front of a bumper 32,968 crowd. With about 30,000 of the spectators supporting Wycombe, it was a party atmosphere for most and the turnout augured well for the club's entry into the League after the greatest season in their 109-year history. With Wycombe having won the Conference by a country mile, while Runcorn only avoided relegation by a couple of points, the Blues were long odds-on to triumph. Runcorn had their moments, but for them to be at Wembley seemed something of a bonus after a difficult season, including a hard passage to the final, while Wycombe were still firing on all cylinders.

If Martin O'Neill's team were not at their most fluent Runcorn rarely troubled them, as they offered evidence of the threat they could pose in the Football League the follow-ing season. Wycombe were given a lift-off by full-back Jason Cousins in the second minute. Runcorn conceded a free-kick twenty yards out, and Cousins, spotting a gap at the end of the precarious Runcorn wall, fired home his first goal of the season.

Runcorn picked themselves up and Steve Shaughnessy forced the first of a series of corners but Steve Thompson continued to probe for Wycombe and it was a foul on the England semi-professional midfielder that led to the Blues' second goal. Up stepped Dave Carroll with a curling free-kick that centre half Andy Kerr headed over Runcorn 'keeper Arthur Williams' despairing leap.

Carroll could have given Wycombe an unassailable lead but he was in two minds with what to do with Thompson's fortieth-minute cross that he lobbed into Williams' hands. And it was Runcorn who bounced back just before the interval. Shaughnessy ran onto Ian Brady's pass from the centre of midfield and raced past Matt Crossley and Kerr before slotting the ball past goalkeeper Paul Hyde.

With Runcorn still looking dangerous, O'Neill brought on Hakan Hayrettin at half-time, freeing Carroll to operate on the right wing. With an anchor in midfield, Wycombe closed Runcorn out and the Linnets began to make sloppy errors.

Wycombe's third goal, in the fifty-ninth minute, once again came from the dead ball, which served them so well throughout the season. Star playmaker Steve Guppy sent over a pinpoint corner to the head of Thompson, who applied the finish. Guppy then came into his own with a series of searing runs, although Runcorn flickered one more time when Ken McKenna's shot hit the inside of the post only to rebound generously for Hyde to scoop away. But Wycombe wrapped up proceedings when a Carroll cross, which Williams seemingly had covered, was instead fumbled into the back of the net.

O'Neill gave a low bow to the supporters after the final whistle. On whether it was a gesture of thanks or farewell, he would not be drawn, fending off suggestions that he was bound for Nottingham Forest. As things turned out, he was to remain loyal to Wycombe for some time yet, and it was to be Wycombe with whom he would return to Wembley the following year to propel them into Division Two.

Runcorn: Williams, Bates, Robertson, Hill, Harold (substitute: Connor), Anderson, Brady (substitute: Parker), Brown, Shaughnessy, McKenna, Brabin.

Wycombe Wanderers: Hyde, Cousins, Cooper, Kerr, Crossley, Thompson, Carroll, Ryan, Hutchinson (substitute: Hayrettin), Scott, Guppy.

In Focus
Trophy Provides League Platform

Wycombe Wanderers were not the first club to take the FA Trophy on the way to Football League membership. Indeed, the statistics show that the trophy is an especially good platform for League status. Seven winners plus another three clubs that have appeared as losing finalists have gone on to enjoy League membership. The very first final was won by Macclesfield Town, who went on to the League seventeen years later – but not before a losing appearance in 1989 and another trophy win in 1996.

Barnet also gave an early hint of what was to come by appearing in the 1972 final and the following year Scarborough and Wigan Athletic, both future League members, contested the final. Boston United and Kidderminster both put in appearances in the 1980s before the League connection really gathered momen-tum the following decade, thanks to Wycombe Wanderers, Colchester United (during their brief non-League stay), Cheltenham Town, Kidderminster and Macclesfield again. Finally, in 2002, Yeovil Town won the trophy the season before promotion.

What brings the 'League connection' about? Almost certainly, first and foremost, the fact that it takes a good side to progress to the trophy final and many of those that do so are eyeing League status. In addition, the trophy gives successful clubs a

Above left: Manager Martin O'Neill acknowledges the fans as he leads his Wycombe Wanderers side out at Wembley.

Above right: Dave Carroll and Jason Cousins celebrate Wycombe's trophy victory.

Right: Action from the final. (Paul Dennis)

massive boost in terms of not only finance but also publicity, with many 'armchair' supporters leaving the comfort of their lounges for a rare stint on the terraces. This in turn gives clubs the boldness required to claim that they are ready for League status and make the necessary investment to do so.

Many other finalists have long harboured League ambitions or could well do so in the future. Woking made all the right noises about going on to the League after their triple trophy success and definitely had the support to do so. Altrincham, Kettering, Telford and Stevenage Borough have all seriously eyed entry to the League, and from another angle ex-League clubs Southport and Barrow both have dreams of a return.

Of course, the beauty of the FA Trophy is that it also throws up the unexpected and there have also been many finalists down the years that are unlikely to reach the heady heights of the Football League. Burscough came out of the blue to win in 2003 and almost certainly do not have the regular fan base to climb above the Unibond League. Others have suffered a sorry demise. Hillingdon Borough and Enfield both once held serious League ambitions. The former, reborn as an entirely new club, will almost certainly never reach such heights, though Enfield, despite all its problems and divisions, is a town that still holds the potential to return to a higher grade of football one day.

Routes to the Final

Runcorn

First round	Hyde United 1, Runcorn 2
Second round	Gloucester City 3, Runcorn 3
Second-round replay	Runcorn 2, Gloucester City 2
Second round, second replay	Gloucester City 0, Runcorn 0
Second round, third replay	Runcorn 4, Gloucester City 1
Third round	Runcorn 1, Winsford United 0
Fourth round	Boston United 0, Runcorn 2
Semi-final, first leg	Runcorn 2, Witton Albion 0
Semi-final, second leg	Witton Albion 1, Runcorn 0

Wycombe Wanderers

First round	Wycombe Wanderers 3, Cheltenham Town 1
Second round	Morecambe 1, Wycombe Wanderers 1
Second-round replay	Wycombe Wanderers 2, Morecambe 0
Third round	Wycombe Wanderers 2, Bromsgrove Rovers 0
Fourth round	Wycombe Wanderers 1, Gateshead 0
Semi-final, first leg	Wycombe Wanderers 2, Sutton United 3
Semi-final, second leg	Sutton United 0, Wycombe Wanderers 4

1994

Woking 2, Runcorn 1
Wembley, 21 May 1994

Two first-half goals, followed by resolute defending, gave Woking victory against eternal FA Trophy bridesmaids Runcorn at a rain-soaked Wembley. Woking supporters made up more than 12,000 of those in the 15,818 crowd, but while it was a triumph for the majority it was exceptionally tough on Runcorn to return north empty handed for the second successive year. Runcorn could not quite match a Woking side that combined the experience of old heads, the young and ambitious and those part-timers who give their all.

Experienced non-League defender Gwynne Berry and former Fulham player Mark Tucker stood firm under the direction of captain Kevan Brown to ensure they kept out Runcorn, who had a wealth of possession but could not match the incisiveness that brought Woking their first-half goals. Even when Berry conceded a penalty for handball, converted by Nigel Shaw in the seventy-fifth minute, Woking's resolve held.

Runcorn started assertively, with Cards 'keeper Laurence Batty holding a header from Andy Lee and Woking's midfield lynchpin Colin Fielder making some crucial interceptions. Woking steadily found their feet, though their twentieth-minute opener did not look on the cards. Dereck Brown failed to forge through the left of the Runcorn defence, but they failed to clear properly and suddenly Scott Steele was through with space to cross. He threaded the ball back to Brown, who swept a left-footed shot past Runcorn 'keeper Arthur Williams and inside the near post.

Ten minutes later Woking were flying. Kevan Brown won possession and moved inside the Runcorn half before knocking the ball forward to Clive Walker. The former Chelsea man showed all his experience with a sweet left-footed chip to the edge of the area. Steele had room and time to control the ball and pull the ball back for Dereck Brown. Brown mishit his shot across goal, but Darran Hay connected to send the ball inside the far post.

Kevin Rattray shows his delight as he proudly holds up his FA Trophy-winners' medal.

Walker crossed for Hay to head narrowly over and they seemed to be coasting, only to be hit by a double injury blow. First Dereck Brown retired with a recurrence of a groin injury, and then Hay, who had strained his knee ligaments, was replaced at half-time. One of those replacements, Kevin Rattray, nearly sealed things for Woking on forty-seven minutes with a backward header from a Walker corner that hit the post. But the enforced changes took the wind out of the Surrey side's sails and they were forced to defend resolutely. Paul Robertson produced a left-footed drive from twenty-five yards that thudded back from the Woking crossbar, but when Mark Tucker's header hit Berry, seemingly on the corner of his chest, referee Paul Durkin gave a penalty. Shaw converted it assuredly.

It was thereafter that Kevan Brown, superb in his covering, became vital amid the Runcorn resurgence. As Dereck Brown and Hay returned to hobble happily with the trophy in front of their appreciative supporters, manager Geoff Chapple declared, 'Now we want to get into the Football League.' Strongly aware of Kidderminster's rejection for promotion because of the Football League's punitive ground-grading deadline, Chapple said, 'Wycombe did it the perfect way: only when they were ready for it.

They took their time before getting a new ground and then went for it. We've been talking about it for two years, the council is holding a reception for us next Saturday and now I hope it backs us.' Chapple, in charge at Woking for ten years, added, 'Ideally, I'd have liked to have played well and won and I've got a bit of sympathy for Runcorn, who played very well and pushed us all the way. But the conditions were difficult and we defended very well and we managed to play some decent football at times.' Runcorn manager John Carroll said, 'I could not have asked any more of my players. We probably needed to score before half-time – Woking got behind the ball, they defended well and their 'keeper did not have a lot of saves to make.'

But at the end, nothing could deny Woking their day of glory – not even Durkin warning them at half-time not to repeat, if they were to score again, their belly-dive celebrations.

Runcorn: Williams, Bates, Lee, Brabin, Robertson, Shaw, Anderson, Connor, McKenna, McInerney (substitute: Hill, 72), Thomas. Substitute (not used): Parker.

Woking: Batty, Berry, K. Brown, Tucker, Wye Clement, D. Brown (substitute: Rattray, 32), Steele, Fielder, Hay (substitute: Puckett, 46), Walker.

In Focus
Runcorn: The Trophy's Nearly Men

Runcorn boast possibly the best trophy record among clubs never to have won the competition. Three losing finals in the space of nine years only tells part of the story. They first gave notice of trophy prowess in 1975/76, when, as a Northern Premier League club, they progressed from the third qualifying round to the semi-finals, only to lose disappointingly 4-0 on aggregate to Stafford Rangers after having had a player sent off early in the second leg.

The 1977/78 season saw another run to the semi-finals but, despite 10 goals in the preceding rounds, again they were unable to score when it really mattered, drawing 0-0 at Altrincham but then losing the return leg 1-0 to a goal scored by Mal Bailey, who had been on their books the previous season. The following campaign saw yet another semi-final appearance and again a narrow semi-final reverse, losing the home leg 2-1 after their goalkeeper broke his leg in the opening minutes and going out despite a gallant 1-1 draw in the away tie despite having had a player sent off early in the game.

After five lean seasons Runcorn, now members of the Conference, overcame Barnet after three replays in the third round, but those exertions had doubtless taken their toll and they crashed out 3-0 at Boston United in the third round.

The first final appearance finally came in 1986 when the Linnets reached the final without recourse to any replays, including a magnificent 2-0 win at Kettering Town in the semi-final second leg, but a fixture backlog caused by the 'big freeze' of 1985/86 caused them to play seven Gola League games in the space of eleven days as well as the final of the Cheshire Senior Cup in the run up to the final, which they lost by a single goal to Altrincham.

Runcorn did not pass the third round again until their 1993 final appearance. It took them four matches and nine goals to get past Gloucester City in the second round and more grit was called for in the semi-finals against Witton Albion. Albion dominated the first leg at Runcorn's Canal Street, but second-half goals from Ken McKenna and Garry Anderson gave the Linnets a vital edge. Runcorn survived a Witton onslaught in the second leg to lose 1-0 but progress to Wembley 2-1 on aggregate, where they were beaten 4-1 by a classy Wycombe Wanderers side.

The road to the 1994 final again saw a stirring semi-final tussle, this time against Unibond League cup fighters Guiseley. Runcorn got off to a flying start at home with a third-minute goal from Ken McKenna, but were stunned when Gary Brabin was sent off in the twenty-fourth minute. Guiseley rallied against ten men and Lutel James set up Calvin Allen to equalise. At Guiseley it was again McKenna who scored, this time the only goal separating the sides coming in extra time after a tense ninety minutes.

Runcorn were relegated to the Unibond League in 1995/96 – the first relegation in the club's history – but still managed to reach the quarter-finals in 1999/2000, losing 2-0 to Telford United.

Routes to the Final

Runcorn

First round	Alfreton Town 0, Runcorn 5
Second round	Runcorn 2, Telford United 1
Third round	Runcorn 1, Halifax Town 1
Third-round replay	Halifax Town 0, Runcorn 2
Fourth round	Gateshead 0, Runcorn 3
Semi-final, first leg	Runcorn 1, Guiseley 1
Semi-final, second leg	Guiseley 0, Runcorn 1

Woking

First round	Bashley 2, Woking 4
Second round	Dagenham & Redbridge 1, Woking 2
Third round	Woking 3, Bromsgrove Rovers 2
Fourth round	Woking 1, Billingham Synthonia 1
Fourth-round replay	Billingham Synthonia 1, Woking 2
Semi-final, first leg	Woking 1, Enfield 1
Semi-final, second leg	Enfield 0, Woking 0
Semi-final replay (at Wycombe Wanderers)	Woking 3, Enfield 0

1995

Woking 2, Kidderminster Harriers 1
Wembley, 14 May 1995

A last-gasp goal from Colin Fielder made Woking the first side since Scarborough in 1977 to retain the FA Trophy. No side could have passed a more rigorous examination in doing so than the Cards did from Kidderminster Harriers. Woking settled the issue in extraordinary fashion, with a goal two minutes from the end of extra time to follow their opener on just fifty-nine seconds.

Mark Tucker, at the far post, headed back a deep corner from the right by Shane Wye to Fielder, who stooped to firmly head the ball in and break Kidderminster's hearts. It was the end of a long haul, after the match had opened spectacularly with a splendid goal for Woking inside the first minute, Scott Steele placing a shot from twenty-five yards beyond Kevin Rose in the Kidderminster goal.

Steele remained majestic for the next twenty minutes, with dribbles and nifty footwork putting Kidderminster on the back foot. Clive Walker, too, was on top form and in the sixth minute he jinked in from the right and unleashed a left-footer that Rose tipped around the post. The Cards were in full flow and looked set for an easy win, but surprisingly the edge to their game slowly faded. Kidderminster, on the other hand, were soon much more into their stride.

Richard Forsyth, Kiddy's stylish link player, and forward Delwyn Humphreys both had shots held by Laurence Batty, whose composure and handling was impeccable throughout the 120 minutes.

Chris Brindley – outstanding in the Kidderminster central defence, along with Paul Webb – twice won headers from Forsyth corners, powering the ball straight at Batty for the first then setting up Paul Davies to head wide. In between, Davies headed in Paul Bancroft's left-wing cross but was ruled to be narrowly offside.

Midfielder Jon Purdie then beat his marker from a throw-in and threaded a stunning pass for Humphreys, who spurned the one glorious chance of the game

Woking's Darran Hay and Chris Brindley of Kidderminster challenge for the ball at Wembley.

by stumbling with only Batty to beat. The 'keeper then saved from Humphreys' diving header – but the deserved equaliser came from the first attack of the second half.

Humphreys, free on the right, turned the ball in to Mark Yates, who drove in a cross-shot, and Paul Davies stabbed out a foot to turn the ball into the net with the scoring instinct of a man claiming his 269th goal in his 571st appearance for the club. Kidderminster's pressurising play was more effective than Woking's neat passing, but it was the Cards who nearly won the match in normal time when Rose arched backwards to tip over a curving twenty-five-yard free-kick from Fielder.

The respect that the sides had proclaimed for each other then stifled further adventure. Even in extra time there were no slips in concentration, until Kidderminster, fatally, left Fielder free. Woking manager Geoff Chapple was somewhat muted in triumph, saying:

> I could not see anything other than 1-1 and I don't think either side deserved to win. I didn't enjoy the game – there were two very tired sides out there… We had a tremendous start and had plenty of possession, but did not ask enough questions. I've got a lot of sympathy for Graham Allner (the Kidderminster manager).

Kidderminster Harriers: Rose, Hodson, Brindley (substitute: Cartwright, 93), Webb, Bancroft, Forsyth, Yates, Deakin, Purdie, Humphreys (substitute: Hughes, 106), Davies.

Woking: Batty Crumplin (substitute: Rattray, 46), Brown, Fielder, Tucker, L. Wye, S. Wye, Ellis, Steele, Walker, Hay (substitute: Newbery, 111).

In Focus
Woking's Hard-Earned Success

Woking not only battled through 120 minutes to retain the FA Trophy, but also became only the third side in twenty-two years to overcome a semi-final first-leg deficit. The opposition was Rushden & Diamonds, now a well-known name in the Football League Division Two, but then a Beazer Homes League side in just their third season following a merger and very much the surprise package of the competition.

Woking just survived a torrid examination in front of a record 4,375 crowd at Diamonds' new flagship Nene Park ground to go back to Woking with a one-goal deficit. After Woking lost captain Kevan Brown with a facial injury, Rushden midfielder Aidy Mann squeezed a shot home through a crowded goalmouth to put the home side in the driving seat. Rushden were sniffing Wembley, but Laurence Batty performed heroics to save from Micky Nuttell, Darren Collins and Ian King, with King also denied by the woodwork.

But though Rushden gave their all in the return at Woking, they were ultimately found wanting in a classic tie. Woking levelled on eighteen minutes when Kevin Rattray fired home. Thereafter, and in contrast to the first leg, it was all Woking and the biggest surprise was that they had to wait until the sixty-seventh minute to find the winner. Scoot Steele put in a delightful first-time ball and Clive Walker showed all his experience to finish with great poise. The only scare came when a Mann chip cleared Batty but John Crumplin was on hand to acrobatically clear from the goal line. Manager Geoff Chapple and his team were chaired from the pitch by hundreds of fans and you would have thought Woking had already won the trophy as they partied long into the night at Kingfield.

Routes to the Final

Kidderminster Harriers

First round	St Albans City 2, Kidderminster Harriers 3
Second round	Kingstonian 0, Kidderminster Harriers 0
Second-round replay	Kidderminster Harriers 1, Kingstonian 0
Third round	Ilkeston Town 2, Kidderminster Harriers 2
Third-round replay	Kidderminster Harriers 2, Ilkeston Town 1
Fourth round	Kidderminster Harriers 5, Altrincham 0
Semi-final, first leg	Kidderminster Harriers 2, Hyde United 0
Semi-final, second leg	Hyde United 1, Kidderminster Harriers 0

Woking

First round	Woking 3, Chesham United 0
Second round	Woking 3, Cheltenham Town 1
Third round	Stevenage Borough 0, Woking 3
Fourth round	Macclesfield Town 0, Woking 1
Semi-final, first leg	Rushden & Diamonds 1, Woking 0
Semi-final, second leg	Woking 2, Rushden & Diamonds 0

1996

Macclesfield Town 3, Northwich Victoria 1
Wembley, 19 May 1996

Tony Hemmings ignored the boo boys and condemned his old club to defeat in the FA Umbro Trophy final. The Northwich Victoria supporters, in a disappointing crowd of 8,672 for the 4 p.m. Sunday kick-off, the lowest for a trophy final, booed Hemmings, for whom Northwich received a record fee of £25,000 when he moved to Wycombe Wanderers in 1983, throughout an engrossing contest. Hemmings, however, simply got on with his business, a mixture of tricks and skills on the left wing, and he had the last laugh with a splendid solo goal that sealed victory for Macclesfield Town. Heartbroken at missing out on two Wembley finals, first with Burton Albion and then with Wycombe Wanderers, the explosive winger was determined to make it third time lucky. Fed by Phil Power, he sprinted seventy yards and calmly placed his shot past Northwich 'keeper Dean Greygoose to settle the all-Cheshire final with nine minutes remaining. It was also a significant moment for Power, returning to the Wembley turf he first graced in 1984 at the age of seventeen as the youngest player ever to appear in a trophy final.

Two minutes later Northwich defender Derek Ward was sent off after committing a second bookable foul on Hemmings. The first had also been on Hemmings just seven minutes earlier. Substituted in the final minute to give Paul Cavell a brief taste of Wembley glory, Hemmings resisted the temptation for any triumphal gesture towards the Vics fans, offering equal applause to both sets of supporters. Hemmings' goal put paid to a second-half Northwich resurgence, after Macclesfield had gone in at the interval two goals to the good. Their first, in the nineteenth minute, was a crisp header by Steve Payne, running onto a long free-kick by Mark Gardiner and shaking off the attention of Ian Cooke, who had been assigned to mark him.

Macclesfield opened up Northwich's defence with some slick long passes and, with twenty-eight minutes gone, went two up with a bizarre own goal. A forty-five-yard ball by Steve Wood found Marc Coates running down the left wing. He delivered his cross early and Northwich defender Dave Burgess, aware that Power was running in behind him, stretched to put the ball out of play only to send it thumping against the stanchion at the back of the net and back into the arms of a beaten and bemused Greygoose.

Northwich attacked vigorously in response. Macclesfield 'keeper Ryan Price turned the ball over the crossbar after a smart shot on the turn by Carwyn Williams. From the resulting corner Steve Walters hit a cross to the far post, where Cooke was unmarked with a gaping goal at which to aim. Sadly for Northwich, he could only hit the far post.

Macclesfield dominated the rest of the half, but Northwich came out after the interval with renewed confidence and were rewarded with a well-worked goal in the fifty-third minute. Walters robbed Hemmings in midfield and played the ball perfectly to the feet of Williams as he ran into the penalty area. He took one pace further and then played the ball past Price.

Chances fell to both sides in the later stages of an increasingly open game, but it was Hemmings who set his stamp on the afternoon and was, unsurprisingly, named Man of the Match. Afterwards, Hemmings said, 'The Northwich fans disappointed me. I only left them to further my career and my transfer fee to Wycombe paid for their new stand.'

Macclesfield Town: Price, Edey, Howarth, Payne, Gardiner, Lyons, Sorvel, Wood (substitute: Hulme, 84), Hemmings (substitute: Cavell, 89), Coates, Power.

Northwich Victoria: Greygoose, Ward, Abel (substitute: Steele, 77), Burgess (substitute: Simpson, 85), Duffy, Williams, Butler, Walters, Vicary, Cooke, Humphreys.

In Focus
No Wembley Glory for Wembley

Macclesfield defender Darren Tinson was cup-tied at Wembley, having appeared for Northwich in the competition earlier in the season. But at least he played in sight of the Twin Towers for Vics when the club won their second-round tie at Wembley FC, who play at Vale Park, within sight of the legendary venue. 'You could see the Twin Towers from the pitch and a lot of the lads were having a laugh telling everyone they were playing at Wembley', Tinson said.

That second-round tie was the closest that Wembley FC ever got to playing at their namesake ground in the trophy final, in the main having to make do with progress through the qualifying stages. However, they can claim to having taken the scalp of trophy winners Kingstonian twice. But it's worth remembering that it is the presence of clubs like Wembley and other minnows of the competition that help give the FA Trophy its charm.

It's a Long Way from Wembley to Wembley – Wembley FC's Trophy Record:

1974/75
Preliminary round   Hayes 1, Wembley 0

1975/76
Preliminary round   Wembley 1, Stevenage Athletic 2

1976/77
Preliminary round   Maidenhead United 1, Wembley 2
First qualifying round   Wembley 0, AP Leamington 2

1977/78
First qualifying round   St Albans City 1, Wembley 2
Second qualifying round   Wembley 2, Bognor Regis Town 2
Second qualifying round, replay   Bognor Regis Town 2, Wembley 0

1978/79
Preliminary round   Wembley 2, Metropolitan Police 1
First qualifying round   Wembley 1, Barnet 1
First qualifying-round replay   Barnet 2, Wembley 3
Second qualifying round   Corinthian Casuals 0, Wembley 4
Third qualifying round   Wembley 0, Dover 3

1979/80
First qualifying round   Wembley 0, Boreham Wood 1

1980/81
Preliminary round   Clapton 1, Wembley 0

1981/82
Preliminary round   Chatham Town 1, Wembley 2
First qualifying round   Harlow Town 1, Wembley 0

1982/83
Preliminary round   Milton Keynes City 0, Wembley 5
First qualifying round   Wembley 2, Harrow Borough 3

1983/84
First qualifying round   Chesham United 1, Wembley 1
First qualifying-round replay   Wembley 4, Chesham United 0
Second qualifying round   Metropolitan Police 1, Wembley 1

Above: Northwich goalkeeper Dean Greygoose looks at the ball in the back of the net as Macclesfield's Marc Coates chases after goalscorer Tony Hemmings.

Left: Steve Walters' right-footed shot just misses the Macclesfield goal.

Second qualifying-round replay	Wembley 2, Metropolitan Police 1
Third qualifying round	Hampton 1, Wembley 1
Third qualifying-round replay	Wembley 0, Hampton 2

1984/85

First qualifying round	Wembley 0, Hornchurch 1

1985/86

Preliminary round	Tilbury 3, Wembley 1

1986/87

First qualifying round	Walthamstow Avenue 0, Wembley 1
Second qualifying round	Kingstonian 0, Wembley 4

Third qualifying round	Wembley 2, Crawley Town 2
Third qualifying-round replay	Crawley Town 1, Wembley 0

1987/88

First qualifying round	Stevenage Borough 2, Wembley 0

1988/89

First qualifying round	Wembley 2, Chelmsford City 1
Second qualifying round	Kingstonian 2, Wembley 0

1989/90

First qualifying round	Wembley 1, St Albans City 0
Second qualifying round	Hitchin Town 1, Wembley 0

1990/91

First qualifying round	Burnham 2, Wembley 2
First qualifying-round replay	Wembley 3, Burnham 1
Second qualifying round	Marlow 5, Wembley 0

1991/92

First qualifying round	Stevenage Borough 2, Wembley 3
Second qualifying round	Wembley 0, Harlow Town 0
Second qualifying-round replay	Harlow Town 0, Wembley 1
Third qualifying round	Wembley 2, Chalfont St Peter 0
First round	Woking 4, Wembley 2

1992/93

Second qualifying round	Wembley 3, Hitchin Town 1
Third qualifying round	Stafford Rangers 1, Wembley 1
Third qualifying-round replay	Wembley 0, Stafford Rangers 1

1993/94

Second qualifying round	Wembley 1, Staines Town 1
Second qualifying-round replay	Staines Town 1, Wembley 0

1994/95

First qualifying round	Wembley 5, Bury Town 2
Second qualifying round	Rushden & Diamonds 2, Wembley 1

1995/96

First qualifying round	Billericay Town 0, Wembley 4
Second qualifying round	Wembley 1, Ruislip Manor 1
Second qualifying-round replay	Ruislip Manor 1, Wembley 2
Third qualifying round	Wembley 2, Bashley 0

First round	Wembley 2, Kingstonian 1
Second round	Wembley 0, Northwich Victoria 2
1996/97	did not enter
1997/98	
First qualifying round	Wembley 2, Gravesend & Northfleet 6
1998/99	
First round	Wembley 1, Witney Town 2
1999/2000	did not enter
2000/01	did not enter
2001/02	did not enter
2002/03	
Qualifying round	Slough Town 2, Wembley 0
First round	Lewes 6, Wembley 4

Routes to the Final

Macclesfield Town

First round	Macclesfield Town 1, Runcorn 0
Second round	Macclesfield Town 2, Purfleet 1
Third round	Macclesfield Town 1, Sudbury Town 0
Fourth round	Gresley Rovers 0, Macclesfield Town 2
Semi-final, first leg	Macclesfield Town 3, Chorley 1
Semi-final, second leg	Chorley 1, Macclesfield Town 1

Northwich Victoria

First round	Hednesford Town 1, Northwich Victoria 1
First-round replay	Northwich Victoria 2, Hednesford Town 0
Second round	Wembley 0, Northwich Victoria 2
Third round	Merthyr Tydfil 1, Northwich Victoria 1
Third-round replay	Northwich Victoria 2, Merthyr Tydfil 2
Third round, second replay	Northwich Victoria 3, Merthyr Tydfil 0
Fourth round	Bromsgrove Rovers 0, Northwich Victoria 1
Semi-final, first leg	Hyde United 1, Northwich Victoria 2
Semi-final, second leg	Northwich Victoria 1, Hyde United 0

1997

Woking 1, Dagenham and Redbridge 0
Wembley, 18 May 1997

Woking won their third FA Umbro Trophy in four years when overcoming dogged ten-man Dagenham & Redbridge before a 24,376 crowd at Wembley. Substitute striker Darran Hay scored the winning goal in the tenth minute of extra time, with a crisp far-post header from a corner by Clive Walker. Hay, winning his third trophy-winners' medal with Woking, had been disappointed to be left out of the starting eleven but had no complaints after his thirteenth goal of the season. It was the second time Hay had grabbed the all-important trophy decider and it was his fifty-third goal for the Conference club. 'This is an absolutely superb feeling', said Hay afterwards. 'I did it at Runcorn and it's great to do it again. The ball already had enough power on it when it came over. I knew that all I had to do was get my head to the ball.' Hay's goal finally broke the stubborn resistance of a Dagenham & Redbridge side who stuck to their task with only ten men after the sending off of Tony Rogers in the sixty-third minute.

Rogers, the Icis League side's veteran striker, was dismissed after tangling with Robin Taylor on the touchline, wrestling him to the ground in an arm lock as they challenged for an innocuous ball. Rogers was shoved by Woking defender Steve Foster, who, in the first half, had been treated for the effects of an elbow in his face from the forward. Daggers' David Pratt joined in and seventeen players flocked to brawl briefly with Rogers proving to be the fall guy after referee Jeff Winter consulted with his linesman.

Woking manager Geoff Chapple believed the sending off paved the way for victory. 'When you are down to ten men on this pitch, you're going to struggle', he said. 'It's very energy-sapping out there. What we had to do then was to use our brains and keep the ball. I thought we did it pretty well.' Indeed, cracks appeared in the Dagenham & Redbridge rearguard and it was left to the magnificent goalkeeping of Paul Gothard to keep Woking at bay. He twice tipped over from Walker and superbly blocked a shot from Taylor, let in by a slip from David Culverhouse, and maintained his defiance in extra time, pushing the ball away at full stretch from Hay to set up the fateful corner. Overall the game was typically British non-League – passionate and committed with the Daggers showing plenty of hustle and bustle but lacking bite in front of goal.

Dagenham had their chances, notably in a brief period after the interval when Steve Conner had Woking 'keeper Laurence Batty scrambling back to stop the ball looping under the bar. A minute later Pratt broke free in the box, but Robin Taylor did just enough to make him scoop his shot over the bar. But any cause for optimism was wiped away ten minutes later with Rogers' dismissal. Woking, who stuck to their pass-and-move principles, had always looked dangerous, with thirty-nine-year-old Walker using all of his know-how to cause Dagenham plenty of problems.

As Dagenham were pushed further back in extra time, a Woking breakthrough looked increasingly likely and it was appropriate that Walker proved the architect. Although the result was not as emphatic as some might have expected – Woking had finished fifth in the Conference with Dagenham & Redbridge fourth in the feeder Icis League – Walker believed his side's class eventually told. 'They just tried to lump it forward and looked for bits and pieces around the box, but they did not have something that was that bit extra special,' said the former Chelsea front man. Veteran Daggers manager Ted Hardy had no grumbles after his side's defeat and revealed that Rogers was a 'broken man' after his sending off. 'Tony is very upset because he thinks he has let the side down', said Hardy. 'But he has been outstanding this season and I can say no more. It's just one of those unfortunate things that happen in football. I have no moans, no grumbles. They scored a very good goal to win it.'

Dagenham & Redbridge: Gothard, Culverhouse, Conner, Creaser, Jacques (substitute: Double, 75), Davidson, Pratt (substitute: Naylor, 81), Parratt, Broom, Rogers, Stimson (substitute: John, 65).

Woking: Batty, Brown, Howard, Foster, Wye, Thompson, (substitute: Jones, 115), Ellis, Taylor, Steele (substitute: L. Wye, 108), Walker, Jackson (substitute: D. Hay, 77).

In Focus
Hardy Proves Evergreen

Dagenham & Redbridge manager Ted Hardy made an extraordinary return to Wembley after a gap of twenty-three years. The sixty-eight-year-old, one of the game's most enduring characters, led Bishop's Stortford out for the last FA Amateur Cup in 1974, a game his side won easily 4–1.

Hardy achieved an immense amount in non-League football since taking his first job with Leyton in 1964. He spent time in charge at Bishop's Stortford, Enfield,

Woking celebrate their remarkable third FA Trophy success.

Leytonstone and Ilford, and Hendon, as well as four separate spells totalling fourteen years in charge at Dagenham. During his amateur football days he guided three of those clubs – Bishop's Stortford, Enfield and Dagenham (twice) to Wembley.

But Hardy thought his management days were over when Dagenham & Redbridge came looking for a saviour towards the end of the 1995/96 season. The seven matches left were not enough to save their place in the Vauxhall Conference, but his work in rebuilding the club was rewarded with the first trophy final appearance by a side from outside the Conference since Leek Town lost to Barrow in 1990. Having also retired from his job at Borough fruit and vegetable market, Hardy, as a part-time manager, found himself putting in as many hours as in any season during his thirty-two-year career. 'In the last three weeks of the season, it was football, football, football and more football', he said. 'We had nine matches in the final thirteen days. We had to use a lot of young players in the reserves and they responded magnificently.'

Hardy not only made history by becoming the oldest manager ever to take a team to Wembley but also laid the foundations for Dagenham & Redbridge returning to the Conference. He steered his side to fourth place again in the Isthmian League in 1997/98, followed by a third placing the following season, during which Hardy announced his retirement on 1 March, leaving the club in a very healthy position.

In the summer of 1999 Garry Hill was appointed as his successor and the Daggers stormed to the championship – and promotion to the Conference – by a massive 24-point margin.

Routes to the Final

Dagenham & Redbridge

Third qualifying round	Aldershot Town 1, Dagenham & Redbridge 3
First round	Dover Athletic 0, Dagenham & Redbridge 2
Second round	Dagenham & Redbridge 2, Chelmsford City 1
Third round	Morecambe 0, Dagenham & Redbridge 0
Fourth round	Dagenham & Redbridge 1, Ashton United 0
Semi-final, first leg	Dagenham & Redbridge 0, Gloucester City 0
Semi-final, second leg	Gloucester City 2, Dagenham & Redbridge 2
Semi-final, replay (at Slough Town)	Dagenham & Redbridge 2, Gloucester City 1

Woking

First round	Wokingham Town 0, Woking 1
Second round	St Albans City 1, Woking 1
Second-round replay	Woking 3, St Albans City 1
Third round	Dorchester Town 2, Woking 3
Fourth round	Heybridge Swifts 0, Woking 1
Semi-final first leg	Woking 1, Stevenage Borough 0
Semi-final, second leg	Stevenage Borough 2, Woking 1
Semi-final replay (at Watford)	Woking 2, Stevenage Borough 1

1998

Cheltenham Town 1, Southport 0
Wembley, 17 May 1998

Cheltenham Town capped a magnificent season by winning the FA Umbro Trophy in roasting heat at Wembley. That the sides were separated by just one goal, scored by Justin Eaton in the eightieth minute, was no surprise. Neither of the Nationwide Conference sides had yielded an inch but neither had been able to impose themselves.

Cheltenham substitute Jim Smith, replacing Clive Walker, set up the situation that ensured that his forty-year-old team-mate would gain his fourth trophy-winner's medal in five years. Smith twisted Kevin Formby inside out and won a free-kick on the right of the area. Fellow substitute Russell Milton sent the ball over flat and fast and the head of full-back Jamie Victory flicked it on to the far post where Eaton, unmarked, guided in a downward header.

It was a game of half chances, where as many fell to Southport as to Cheltenham. Cheltenham goalkeeper Steve Book beat down a left-foot shot by Kevin Formby after a fine crossfield ball from Ged Kielty. Brian Ross shot over the bar after a neat move, Brian Butler had the ball taken off his toe after Dave Thompson had laid it into his path and Formby failed to get in a shot when left clear.

The influence of Southport player-manager Paul Futcher, indestructible at forty-one, was clear. He was simple, with no-risk defending and no extravagance. But even he could not resist just before half-time. Forty yards from goal, a clearance from a corner dropped to him. He swung in a volley but the ball skewed off wildly to the right.

Managerial honours instead went to Cheltenham's Steve Cotterill. At thirty-three, he was the youngest to lead a side to a Wembley victory with the exception of Roy McDonough, who took Colchester to the trophy in 1992 as player-manager. Cotterill saw glimpses of the form that had taken Cheltenham to second place in the Conference and the FA Cup third round, but it was enough.

Cheltenham manager Steve Cotterill shows off the trophy.

Another FA Trophy success for the evergreen Clive Walker.

An intelligent flick by Eaton from a pass by Bob Bloomer supplied Dale Watkins with the best opening of the match, smothered bravely by Southport 'keeper Billy Stewart. Early on Watkins crossed to Eaton and his knock back to Darren Knight was blasted high and wide.

Cheltenham were screaming for a penalty – not given – when Eaton was stopped by a muscular challenge and a bit of shirt tugging. Stewart punched a Knight cross onto Walker's head and the veteran striker did well to direct his header with some pace back toward the 'keeper, but it dropped handily back to the back-pedalling Stewart.

The Robins should have taken the lead in the second half when good work down the left by Knight set up Watkins, but his left foot missed the kick altogether. As the game began to drift Walker got in his only telling run of the match when his long floated cross was kicked away by Futcher. But it was the late arrival of Smith and Milton on which the game turned.

Since his appointment as Cheltenham manager in February 1997, initially as caretaker, Cotterill led Cheltenham back into the Conference from the Dr Martens League and turned them immediately into Conference heavyweights. That his side deserved this silverware could not be questioned. When 10,000 Robins fans gathered to greet their heroes' homecoming, Cotterill took a back seat, leaving it up to the players to soak up the accolades, but in the end gave in to constant pressure from the fans and got the biggest cheer of the night as he held the trophy aloft.

Cheltenham Town: Book, Duff, Banks, Freeman, Victory, Knight, Bloomer, Howells, Walker, Eaton, Watkins. Used substitutes: Smith, Milton.

Southport: Stewart, Horner, Futcher, Ryan, Farley, Kielty, Butler, Gamble, Formby, Thompson, Ross. Used substitutes: Whittaker, Bollard.

In Focus
Wembley – Venue of Veterans

The 1998 FA Umbro Trophy final will largely be remembered for the participation of two of the game's enduring figures on the pitch – Clive Walker and Paul Futcher. For Walker, it was an extraordinary return to collect his fourth FA Trophy-winner's medal following three as a player with Woking. In fact, Walker's association with Wembley goes back to 1973, when he was on the substitutes' bench for the England *v*. Germany schoolboys' international.

Chelsea was to be Walker's home for the best part of a decade. He was a first team regular from 1977 to 1983, contributing 65 goals in 224 appearances, including an unstoppable left-foot strike that helped Chelsea knock Liverpool out of the FA Cup in 1978, etching his name in Stamford Bridge folklore in the process.

In 1984 he moved to Sunderland for a season, where he again played at Wembley in the Milk Cup final, but he was on the losing side and hit the post with a penalty.

After spells at Queens Park Rangers, Fulham and Brighton, Walker found his way to Woking, for whom he scored 91 goals in four years, taking them to three Wembley finals. In 1999 he became the first player ever to have scored 100 goals in both League and non-League football whilst playing for Cheltenham.

Southport's player-manager Paul Futcher became a well-known face in English football, playing for a number of clubs during a long League career and also collecting eleven England Under-21 caps. The defender began his career as an apprentice with his hometown club Chester in July 1973, playing twenty-one times in the first team before a £100, 000 move to Luton the following summer. After 131 games he moved to Manchester City for £350,000, where he made 30 appearances in his debut season, but things didn't work out the following season and he moved on to Oldham Athletic before becoming something of a 'gun for hire' with spells at Derby County, Barnsley, Halifax Town and Grimsby Town.

Futcher cut his managerial teeth at Gresley Rovers, guiding them to the DR Martens League title, but with their ground not up to Conference standards, he made the move to Southport in the summer of 1997, immediately guiding them to the trophy final.

Routes to the Final

Cheltenham Town

First round	Enfield 1, Cheltenham Town 1
First-round replay	Cheltenham Town 5, Enfield 1
Second round	Cheltenham Town 3, Rushden & Diamonds 1
Third round	Ashton United 0, Cheltenham Town 1
Fourth round	Cheltenham Town 1, Hayes 0
Semi-final, first leg	Cheltenham Town 2, Dover Athletic 1
Semi-final, second leg	Dover Athletic 2, Cheltenham Town 2

Southport

First round	Southport 3, Winsford United 0
Second round	Yeading 0, Southport 6
Third round	Altrincham 0, Southport 2
Fourth round	Grantham Town 1, Southport 1
Fourth-round replay	Southport 3, Grantham Town 1
Semi-final, first leg	Slough Town 0, Southport 1
Semi-final, second leg	Southport 1, Slough Town 1

1999

Kingstonian 1, Forest Green Rovers 0
Wembley, 15 May 1999

Tarkan Mustafa responded to a half-time dressing down for his Kingstonian side with the goal that sealed manager Geoff Chapple's fourth FA Trophy win in six seasons. Three times Chapple had lifted the FA Trophy with Woking – 'the other club' as Kingstonian officials, at pain of fines, had forced him to call it – and it was his magic touch that again produced a winning response from the Kingstonian players. 'I had to say some unrepeatable things to them at half-time', admitted Chapple. 'We were lucky to still be in with a chance. I was seething, but they made me proud in the end even though it wasn't the best of games.'

Indeed, Forest Green set the tempo after kick-off as Marc McGregor and Alex Sykes taunted the Ks with their pace. It was McGregor who nearly put Rovers in the lead when he beat Kingstonian skipper Matt Crossley and shot inside the near post, but goalkeeper Steve Farrelly dropped to his right to palm the ball around the post. This proved a pivotal moment, as many Rovers supporters maintained that their side should have earned a penalty for a tug on McGregor's shirt.

Rovers were commanding in defence, restricting Kingstonian's talismanic striker David Leworthy to one half-chance, when a firm volley from Geoff Pitcher's lay-off was held by Justin Shuttlewood, who had overcome an injury sustained in the semi-finals to return between the posts.

David Mehew lobbed over from twenty-five yards as Forest Green ended the first half the stronger side, but whatever Chapple said to his players during half-time had the desired effect, as Kingstonian instantly raised their game. Defender Mark Harris centred from the left, Gary Patterson pressured Shuttlewood, who spilt it for Mustafa to volley in from the edge of the box. With the cushion of a goal, the Kingstonian midfield duo of Patterson and Man of the Match Geoff Pitcher increasingly controlled the middle of the park and only some casual finishing prevented Ks from extending their lead.

Rovers tried to respond and manager Frank Gregan sent on Rob Cook and Steve Winter on the hour, replacing Chris Honor and Nathan Wigg, but a brief spell of pressure failed to get reward. Farrelly was, as ever, dominant in the air, and provided Kingstonian with security at the back. The final minutes were predictably frantic, as Forest Green pushed forward for an equaliser to take them to extra time, but Ks managed to retain enough composure to hold them off.

'We can do better', Chapple reflected, 'but I promised that we'd bring the trophy back to Kingstonian, the players have done that and you can't be too critical.' Gregan, meanwhile, made it clear that Shuttlewood should not blame himself for the defeat. 'He probably dropped three crosses all season, and that was one of them,' Gregan said. 'He's earned us about 20 points over the season and has been responsible for us playing Conference football next season.'

Forest Green: Shuttlewood, Hedges, Forbes, Bailey, Kilgour, Wigg, Honor, Drysdale, McGregor, Mehew, Sykes. Substitutes: Cook, Winter, Smart, Coupe, Perrin.

Kingstonian: Farrelly, Mustafa, Luckett, Crossley, Stewart, Harris, Patterson, Pitcher, Rattray, Leworthy, Akuamoah. Substitutes: Francis, John, Corbett, Smith, Trantor.

In Focus
Forest Green's Unique Double

May 1999 saw Forest Green Rovers become the first club to reach the finals of both the FA Vase and FA Trophy. Whereas Rovers lifted the Vase in 1982, on this occasion they had to suffer the disappointment of missing out on the big prize. But, despite the end result, the afternoon was a terrific occasion for those who travelled from Gloucestershire, the match being little short of a celebration in honour of the team that everyone thought were certain to be relegated at the end of their first season in the Conference, yet ultimately finished in a respectable twelfth position.

Reorganisation within the structure of the competition meant that the FA granted exemption for all Conference clubs to the second round of the competition for 1998/99. Seven matches stood between Rovers and a trip to Wembley.

Boreham Wood and Witney Town found themselves embarrassed by their Conference hosts as they both conceded four goals, but Green finally encountered stubborn opposition in the following rounds at Weymouth and Hitchin Town. The latter were a particularly gutsy outfit and included future Cambridge United striker Zema Abbey in their line-up. After conceding two goals within as many minutes they recovered to match their opponents for the remainder of the tie, although Rovers' Alex Sykes will never forget his second-half miss as he rounded the 'keeper and fired wide from ten yards.

A quarter-final tie with previous season's finalists Southport passed in a blur, as Rovers made their visitors look ordinary. Then came what was the most memorable clash of the cup run, a two-legged semi-final tie with St Albans City. Future

Dagenham & Redbridge boss Garry Hill was manager of Saints at the time and went out of his way with the mind games before the actual tie took place, including a fifteen-minute kick-off delay at Clarence Park for the first leg, officially due to crowd congestion. Rovers really should have gone on to wrap up the first leg after being awarded a penalty within seconds of the kick-off. Jason Drysdale converted the spot kick but Saints equalised before half-time and Rovers' hearts were in their mouths as the Ryman Leaguers maintained their pressure.

All seemed over for Rovers in the second leg as they went two goals behind in the opening minutes of the first half, before an extraordinary fightback to take Green to Wembley. Alex Sykes reduced the deficit for Green on the stroke of half-time, but St Albans held firm until the seventy-sixth minute. David Mehew twice had shots blocked but the ball fell to Ian Hedges, who drilled home the equaliser from five yards.

Roared on by the majority of the 3,002 crowd, it was substitute Gary Smart who grabbed the winner. The thirty-six-year-old former Bath City stalwart latched onto a Mehew pass and lashed the ball home with the aid of a slight deflection. Forest Green goalkeeper Steve Perrin made a spectacular fingertip save to prevent a St Albans equaliser in the dying seconds, and Green were on their way to Wembley again.

Kingstonian captain Matt Crossley proudly displays the FA Trophy.

Routes to the Final

Forest Green Rovers

Second round	Forest Green Rovers 4, Boreham Wood 1
Third round	Forest Green Rovers 4, Witney Town 0
Fourth round	Weymouth 1, Forest Green Rovers 2
Fifth round	Hitchin Town 1, Forest Green Rovers 2
Sixth round	Forest Green Rovers 4, Southport 1
Semi-final, first leg	St Albans City 1, Forest Green Rovers 1
Semi-final, second leg	Forest Green Rovers 3, St Albans City 2

Kingstonian

Second round	Gloucester City 1, Kingstonian 2
Third round	Kingstonian 5, Kettering Town 2
Fourth round	Whyteleafe 0, Kingstonian 3
Fifth round	Kingstonian 1, Yeovil Town 0
Sixth round	Northwich Victoria 0, Kingstonian 2
Semi-final, first leg	Kingstonian 2, Cheltenham Town 2
Semi-final, second leg	Cheltenham Town 1, Kingstonian 3

2000

Kingstonian 3, Kettering Town 2
Wembley, 13 May 2000

This had it all. A five-goal thriller played in brilliant sunshine saw Kingstonian retain the FA Trophy in the last final to be played at the soon-to-be-condemned Wembley Stadium. It was a personal triumph for Kingstonian boss Geoff Chapple, who stamped himself as a trophy specialist by getting his hands on the cup for the fifth time in just seven years. Two-goal Eddie Akuamoah, Kingstonian's longest-serving player, and French ace Amara Simba sealed victory for Ks, but Tarkan Mustafa was the driving force behind the Surrey side's victory.

Despite sweltering heat, Kingstonian showed little sign that they had played 6 matches in nine days leading up to the final. It was Mustafa who initially brought the game to life with a twenty-five-yard shot curling wide of Kettering 'keeper Adam Sollitt's left-hand post. But Kettering soon got into gear, notably thanks to former Cheltenham striker Dale Watkins, who went close with both a header and free-kick as well as looking like the Poppies' most dangerous provider.

The pendulum began to swing towards Kingstonian as the first half wore on, with former England semi-professional midfielder Geoff Pitcher and Eddie Akuamoah running at the Poppies' defence. Pitcher put in two superb right-wing runs but his delivery was lacking.

Then, on forty-one minutes, Amara Simba produced a superb pass with a subtle flick and Eddie Akuamoah used his pace to outwit the Kettering defence and side-foot the ball into the net from fifteen yards for a 1-0 lead. The Surrey side finished the half on top as Akuamoah and Mustafa combined and Akuamoah's shot-cum-cross was hacked off the line for a corner by defender Steve Perkins.

But if anyone thought the second half was going to be a cakewalk for Ks, they were mistaken. On fifty-five minutes, Kingstonian gave away a free-kick from thirty-five yards out. Carl Adams' ball found Colin Vowden on the back post, whose header

Let the celebrations begin! Kingstonian captain Matt Crossley is in party mood.

deflected off Ks captain Matt Crossley and past goalkeeper Steve Farrelly to level the score.

Kettering thought they were in front shortly afterwards. Substitute Lee Hudson caused panic in the Kingstonian defence and after a Ks mix-up Hudson shot into an empty net and ran away twirling his shirt around his head. But the linesman had raised his flag deeming Hudson to be offside. It appeared to be a tough decision for Kettering.

Nevertheless, Kettering's bad luck evened out just five minutes later. Brett McNamara made it into the penalty box on the goal side of Mustafa but lost his footing and fell to the floor. Referee Mr Dunn pointed to the spot but television replays showed that the match official had got it badly wrong. Craig Norman's cunning spot kick had Farrelly, already diving to his left, bamboozled as the ball trickled into the opposite side of the net to give Kettering a sixty-fifth minute lead.

Five minutes later, Ks were level. A free-kick from the halfway line was only headed upwards by Kettering defender Chris Perkins. Ks defender Mark Harris nodded the ball down to Akuamoah, who hit the ball into the roof of the net from six yards.

Both sides spurned further chances before Simba sealed victory for Kingstonian. Mustafa, on his way to the Man of the Match award, set off on a dazzling forty-yard run before shooting. Sollitt spilled his shot and Simba was on hand to slot the ball home from ten yards. Geoff Pitcher could have widened the margin in the last minute, but shot straight at Sollitt. It didn't matter. Chapple's wonders had done it again.

Kettering Town: Sollitt, McNamara, Adams, Perkins, Vowden, Norman (Diuk), Fisher, Brown, Shutt, Watkins (Hudson), Setchell (Hopkins). Substitutes (not used): Ridgway, Wilson.

Kingstonian: Farrelly, Mustafa, Luckett, Crossley, Stewart (Saunders), Harris, Kadi (Leworthy), Pitcher, Green (Basford), Simba, Akuamoah. Substitutes (not used): Hurst, Allan.

In Focus
Goodbye Wembley

The 2000 FA Trophy final was one of the last games to be played at the old Wembley Stadium before its closure and eventual demolition over two years later. While a new stadium is springing from the rubble, the absence of a national stadium in the meantime was a hard blow to the trophy. It undoubtedly had an adverse effect on attendances in the rounds leading up to the final, as the carrot had always been the prospect of a Wembley final.

The destruction of Wembley was carried out with undue haste and is almost certainly something that future generations will be left to repent over, with nothing left but match programmes and a few items of memorabilia being auctioned on the internet, plus archive footage and images such as the ones within this book. A new national stadium was needed, but for it to be at Wembley was not essential. Wembley could have been preserved for future generations, just as the Berlin 1936 Olympic Stadium and Stockholm 1912 Olympic Stadium have been – superb living 'museums' and architectural monuments.

Wembley earned Grade II Listed status from English Heritage but this proved no guarantee of preservation, making a mockery of the listing process. With its Roman coliseum style of the exterior arches, numerous ornamental fixtures and, above all, the Towers themselves – recognised worldwide as the home and emblem of football – Wembley was one of the world's most beautiful and historic grounds. From its memorable opening in 1923 when it hosted Bolton Wanderers' 2-0 FA Cup final victory over West Ham United in what became known as the 'White Horse Final', Wembley has been steeped in history.

Among the many epic FA Cup finals the greatest was probably the 'Matthews Final' of 1953, in which Stanley Matthews wreaked havoc down the right wing. His Blackpool team were 3-1 down to Bolton Wanderers with twenty-two minutes to go and trailing 3-2 with two minutes on the clock, before roaring back for a thrilling 4-3 victory – Stan Mortensen scoring a hat-trick. That same year, Wembley hosted probably England's most numbing defeat in their footballing history when they were outclassed by Ferenc Puskas' Hungary in a 6-3 defeat at Wembley. Thirteen years later Wembley would host the greatest ever moment for English football, when the World Cup was lifted below the Royal Box after one of the most dramatic finals.

The FA Trophy, FA Amateur Cup and FA Vase all gave clubs and their players a chance to play at Wembley that would otherwise have been a distant dream. What is most tragic is that no middle ground was reached that allowed for the preservation of the Twin Towers. Apparently they were cast out of ferro-concrete and might have crumbled beneath any effort to move them. However, no attempt to do this was ever even initiated.

A new stadium beckons – but sadly, one ingredient it will lack is any sense of history.

Routes to the Final

Kingstonian
Second round	Folkestone Invicta 0, Kingstonian 1
Third round	Wealdstone 0, Kingstonian 5
Fourth round	Kingstonian 2, Moor Green 1
Fifth round	Yeovil Town 0, Kingstonian 1
Sixth round	Kingstonian 0, Southport 0
Sixth-round replay	Southport 0, Kingstonian 1
Semi-final, first leg	Sutton United 1, Kingstonian 1
Semi-final, second leg	Kingstonian 6, Sutton United 0

Kettering Town
Second round	Kettering Town 2, Thame United 2
Second-round replay	Thame United 0, Kettering Town 1
Third round	Kettering Town 2, Welling United 0
Fourth round	Kettering Town 2, Walton and Hersham 2
Fourth-round replay	Walton and Hersham 0, Kettering Town 2
Fifth round	Workington 0, Kettering Town 1
Sixth round	Kettering Town 2, Bishop Auckland 2
Sixth-round replay	Bishop Auckland 0, Kettering Town 2
Semi-final, first leg	Kettering Town 1, Telford United 0
Semi-final, second leg	Telford United 0, Kettering Town 0

2001

Canvey Island 1, Forest Green Rovers 0
Villa Park, 13 May 2001

Ben Chenery was Canvey Island's hero after the Ryman League side upset Conference opponents Forest Green Rovers to win the FA Umbro Trophy at Villa Park. Canvey Island could easily have been jaded from a nightmare run of matches during the final week of their season. Their success in the trophy and a second-round appearance in the FA Cup meant they played 12 games in thirteen days to complete their fixtures. But their tired legs were rejuvenated in the sixteenth minute when Forest Green paid the price for some lacklustre defending.

Chenery scored his first goal of the season from Canvey Island's first corner of the match. Mark Stimson's centre, which followed a well-rehearsed short-corner, floated over to Chenery, who took advantage of some slack marking from the Forest Green defence and rose unchallenged to power his header past goalkeeper Steve Perrin.

Forest Green had six players cup-tied and their play never really flowed. Former Aston Villa winger Tony Daley was expected to provide their attacking impetus, but, aside from a mazy run at the start of the game, he was a largely anonymous presence on his return to his old stamping ground. Canvey, on the other hand, settled down quickly, and looked even more assertive once they had taken the lead. Steve Parmenter went close to doubling Canvey's lead as he made a penetrating run from the midfield but Perrin was equal to his shot, diving to his right.

Forest Green pushed Jason Drysdale forward in an attempt to liven their game up, but the switch to three centre-backs seemed to hinder rather than help their cause. Indeed, it took a superb tackle from Adam Lockwood to stop Wayne Vaughan in his tracks.

Daley switched flanks after the interval, with Frankie Bennett coming on to play on the right. Some stern words at half-time from Forest Green boss Nigel Spink, making a Villa Park homecoming, had clearly shaken them from their lethargy.

But an increase in possession was not delivering any clear-cut goalscoring opportunities.

Meanwhile, Canvey still looked dangerous and Chris Duffy worked his way into the box, but his shot was blocked and Parmenter blazed wildly over the bar from the rebound. But for the last twenty minutes Canvey sat back, the pressure built and the Conference side started to take a grip on the game.

Above: The players start to celebrate the victory.

Left: Goalscorer Ben Chenery displays the cup.

(Both courtesy of Ian Walmsley and Geoff Barsby)

Adie Foster headed over from Martin Foster's cross, when he should have levelled the score. Then Daley's long-range effort was well saved by Ashley Harrison, as Canvey continued to stand firm. With fifteen minutes remaining Rovers brought on Paul Hunt as they intensified their efforts to score an equaliser. Two years earlier it was his goal that kept Rovers in the Conference, but his contribution this time was less impacting.

As Rovers continued to press, they left themselves open to the counter-attack and Canvey should have eased their nerves with a second goal with five minutes left to play. John Kennedy's low cross sat up for Neil Gregory and he struck the ball sweetly on the volley, but high of the goal. But former Ipswich midfielder John Kennedy maintained Canvey's composure during an occasionally ill-tempered second half, from which both sides were lucky to emerge without a sending off.

Canvey Island: Harrison, Kennedy, Duffy, Chenery, Bodley, Ward, Tilson, Stimson, Gregory, Vaughan, Parmenter. Substitutes: Bennett, Jones, Adam Miller, Tanner, Ian Thompson.

Forest Green: Perrin, Cousins, Lockwood, Martin Foster, Clark, Burns, Daley, Drysdale, Adrian Foster, Meechan, Slater. Substitutes: Hunt, Hedges, Bennett, Prince, Ghent.

In Focus
Jeff is King of Canvey

Canvey Island's history dates back to 1926 – but its glory years have been over the past few seasons under the guidance of manager Jeff King. King, a former Canvey Island player, took over the reins in 1992 when the club was in the Essex Senior League. His impact was immediate, with Canvey winning the league title in 1992/93 and reaching the semi-finals of the FA Vase. Canvey Island gained promotion to the Isthmian League in 1994 and won promotion from Division Three and Division Two in successive seasons. In 1995/96 they reached the FA Cup first round and drew 2-2 with Brighton & Hove Albion at Park Lane in front of a record crowd of 3,500. The replay was lost at Brighton before a gate of over 7,000.

Canvey surprisingly suffered relegation in 1996/97, but bounced back with the Division Two Championship the following season. In 1998/99 the club won promotion to the Premier Division of the Ryman League – but the real fun had only just started. The 2000/01 campaign was Canvey's most memorable to date and stamped them as one of the best-known non-League sides outside the Conference. Initially this was earned in the FA Cup, as the Islanders, drawn at home to Port Vale in the first round, drew 4-4 in an extraordinary game.

Vale cruised into a 2-0 lead and missed a penalty and, despite a Canvey fightback, Vale were 4-2 up with two minutes to go, but Andy Jones and Wayne Vaughan scored to level the tie. Then they really hit the headlines by winning at Port Vale by

2–1 after extra time, where a wonderful run and finish from Wayne Vaughan sealed matters, earning a home tie with local rivals Southend United. The massive local interest meant that the tie was switched to Roots Hall, and 11,402 people witnessed a 2–1 defeat for Canvey.

However, an even more remarkable run in the FA Trophy saw the Gulls defy pre-tournament odds of 66–1 to win the trophy and become the first non-Conference side to do so since Bishop's Stortford in 1981. To win the FA Trophy they had to beat four Conference teams in succession – Stevenage Borough, Telford United, Chester City and Forest Green.

In 2001/02 Canvey reached the FA Cup third round for the first time. Canvey stunned ambitious Wigan Athletic in the first round at JJB Stadium, with Neil Gregory scoring a magnificent eighty-third-minute volley. The win earned them a home tie with Northampton Town, where a packed Park Lane saw Gregory again the hero, firing home from close range after a swift Canvey attack started by former West Ham defender Julian Dicks. BBC Sport Online acclaimed both of Gregory's goals as Goals of the Week.

An away tie to Burnley was the reward, where, in front of 11,496 fans, Canvey bravely went down 4–1 but won a standing ovation from the Burnley fans.

Routes to the Final

Canvey Island

Second round	Harlow Town 2, Canvey Island 2
Second-round replay	Canvey Island 2, Harlow Town 0
Third round	Canvey Island 5, Northwood 1
Fourth round	Bilston Town 0, Canvey Island1
Fifth round	Canvey Island 1, Stevenage Borough 1
Fifth-round replay	Stevenage Borough 0, Canvey Island 0
	(Canvey Island won 4-2 on penalties.)
Sixth round	Canvey Island 1, Telford United 0
Semi-final, first leg	Canvey Island 2, Chester City 0
Semi-final, second leg	Chester City 0, Canvey Island 2

Forest Green Rovers

Third round	Forest Green Rovers 6, Barton Rovers 1
Fourth round	Matlock Town 2, Forest Green Rovers 2
Fourth-round replay	Forest Green Rovers 3, Matlock Town 1
Fifth round	Forest Green Rovers 2, Rushden & Diamonds 0
Sixth round	Forest Green Rovers 2, Worksop Town 1
Semi-final, first leg	Forest Green Rovers 2, Hereford United 2
Semi-final, second leg	Hereford United 1, Forest Green Rovers 4

2002

Yeovil Town 2, Stevenage Borough 0
Villa Park, 12 May 2002

Yeovil Town deservedly lifted the FA Trophy for the first time after a goal in each half gave them victory over Stevenage Borough. Carl Alford and Man of the Match Adam Stansfield were the heroes for Yeovil, as they gave an overture to promotion to the Football League the following season.

For the first ten minutes, however, the Hertfordshire team looked likely winners, never more so than after thirty seconds when, after Yeovil's England non-League international Anthony Tonkin had carelessly given the ball away, Kirk Jackson met Jean-Michel Sigere's cross with a looping header. There could have been no better way for Chris Weale, Yeovil's nineteen-year-old goalkeeper, to settle his nerves than with the magnificent flying save he made to tip the ball over the crossbar for a corner.

However, Yeovil settled down after that early scare with Alford and Stansfield starting to cause problems for the Stevenage defence. And on twelve minutes Yeovil were in front. Adam Lockwood launched a long throw into the penalty area that Stevenage failed to clear and Alford, with his back to goal, executed a brilliant overhead scissor-kick. For Alford it was a moment to savour, as he had been on the losing Witton Albion side back in the 1992 trophy final.

Yeovil moved into top gear and Alford assumed the role of creator as he put Stansfield through. But Stansfield dawdled and his shot was smothered away for a corner. Stansfield then supplied a penetrating cross that the oncoming Alford would surely have dispatched had Stevenage 'keeper Paul Wilkerson not palmed the ball onto his own crossbar and out of harm's way.

Despite flashes of skill by Sigere, Stevenage were limited to speculative long-range efforts, with Simon Wormull trying his luck on a couple of occasions. Stevenage opened the second half with plenty of possession still, but failing to make any telling inroads. Yeovil, however, were battling for everything and they looked menacing on the break, with the speed of Stansfield causing countless problems for the Stevenage defence, while Alford was producing his best performance for the Glovers since arriving at Huish Park the previous summer. It was only a matter of time before Gary Johnson's side doubled their lead and Stansfield was rewarded for his endeavour, dispatching a low shot through Wilkerson's legs after an Alford flick on.

Alford could have made it 3-0 when he missed a glorious chance as he placed his shot into the side netting from close range, while Lee Johnson had two great opportunities. The first saw him whip in a terrific twenty-five-yard free-kick which was tipped over the bar and he then completely messed up a shot which sailed over the top when it would have been easier to have got it on target.

For Stevenage, midfielder Lee Johnson, the son of the victorious manager, must have run Adam Stansfield close in the voting for the Man-of-the-Match award, as did the energetic Simon Wormull. Too often, though, Stevenage's approach was one-dimensional and they failed to break down a solid defence marshalled by Colin Pluck and Terry Skiverton and second-half substitute Tom White.

Delighted Yeovil manager Gary Johnson said, 'The club and the fans have been waiting for more than thirty years to win this and now we have won it for them. I'm delighted.' Stevenage boss Wayne Turner was gracious in defeat, saying, 'Yeovil have got to be the favourites next year to go up. They have got it all in place, the twenty-four players, the ground and the finances. They are a very good outfit at this level.'

Turner's prediction was to be emphatically proved correct.

Stevenage: Wilkerson, Hamsher, Goodliffe, Trott, Fraser, Fisher, Wormull, Evers, Jackson, Sigere, Clarke. Substitutes: Stirling, Dudley Campbell, Jamie Campbell, Greygoose, Williams.

Yeovil: Weale, Lockwood, Tonkin, Skiverton, Pluck, Way, Stansfield, Johnson, Alford, Crittenden, McIndoe. Substitutes: White, Sheffield, O'Brien, Giles, Lindegaard.

In Focus
Floodgates of Success Open for Yeovil

Yeovil's FA Trophy success was to prove the springboard for the club's elevation to Football League status the following year. Indeed, until 2002, the biggest surprise was not only that Yeovil were still a non-League club, but also that they had never won the FA Trophy or appeared in the final.

Yeovil's sum of qualities as a club were practically unsurpassed at non-League level: year in, year out attendance levels way ahead of other clubs, an almost continuous spell amongst non-League's elite and string of good FA Cup runs and giant-killings. Small wonder that Yeovil made no less than twenty-eight applications to join the Football League prior to the introduction of automatic promotion in 1986/87, only failing by three votes to oust Workington in 1976.

Carl Alford scores with an overhead kick to put Yeovil ahead. (Adrian Hopper)

Created as the Yeovil Casuals in 1895, the club merged with Petters United in 1914 to become Yeovil and Petters United. They moved to the Huish in 1920, joined the Southern League soon after and made their first Football League application in 1927. Dropping the 'Petters United' for 'Town' after the Second World War, Yeovil announced their presence to a wider audience in 1948/49. After beating Division Two Bury, a record all-ticket crowd of 16,318 saw them beat Sunderland on the famous sloping pitch in the FA Cup third round. In the fourth round Yeovil lost away to Manchester United in front of an 81,565 crowd at Maine Road, as Old Trafford was still not in use due to war damage.

The Southern League Championship and Cup double followed in 1954/55 and the league title was taken again in 1964/65 and 1970/71. As league runners-up in the 1969/70 and 1972/73 seasons, coupled with a string of FA Cup exploits, Yeovil deservedly took their place as one of the founding clubs in the Alliance Premier League in 1979. This step up did not bear the expected fruits. Yeovil struggled and, after a couple of flirtations, they were relegated to the Isthmian League after a catastrophic season in 1984/85.

Yeovil were Isthmian League runners-up two years running before winning the title and returning to the Conference in 1987/88 with 91 and 92 points respectively, but they went one better at the third attempt, winning the Premier Division title in 1987/88.

In 1990 Yeovil left their famous sloping Huish ground to go to Huish Park, a ground easily fit for Football League use. However, they once again faced relegation in 1995. Still enjoying tremendous support way ahead of their rivals, Yeovil won the Isthmian League in 1996/97, with 8,007 watching the game against Enfield.

In 2000/01 Yeovil gave their biggest hint yet that the Football League was looming, pushing the moneyed Rushden & Diamonds all the way and reaching the FA Cup third round. The following season saw a rather frustrating campaign as far as the title race was concerned. The club was again in the race for the championship, only to falter towards the end as the twin attentions of league and the FA Trophy took their toll.

The following season there was no such error, as Yeovil stormed to the Nationwide Conference title – and promotion to the Football League – by 17 points, being unbeaten at home. The only shock at Huish Park came in the FA Trophy when eventual winners Burscough stunned the Glovers with a 2-0 win.

Routes to the Final

Stevenage Borough

Third round	Stevenage Borough 5, Dover Athletic 1
Fourth round	Stevenage Borough 1, Bashley 0
Fifth round	Stevenage Borough 3, Forest Green Rovers 2
Sixth round	Stevenage Borough 1, Stalybridge 0
Semi-final, first leg	Morecambe 1, Stevenage Borough 2
Semi-final, second leg	Stevenage Borough 2, Morecambe 0

Yeovil Town

Third round	Tiverton Town 1, Yeovil Town 3
Fourth round	Yeovil Town 1, Doncaster Rovers 1
Fourth-round replay	Doncaster Rovers 4, Yeovil Town 5
Fifth round	Yeovil Town 2, Canvey Island 1
Sixth round	Northwich Victoria 0, Yeovil Town 2
Semi-final, first leg	Yeovil Town 4, Burton Albion 0
Semi-final, second leg	Burton Albion 2, Yeovil Town 1

2003

Burscough 2, Tamworth 1
Villa Park, 18 May 2003

Burscough completed the biggest FA Trophy shock of all time by beating Tamworth in by far the biggest day of the club's fifty-seven-year history. The Unibond League side, with normal home gates of around 170, defied pre-tournament odds of 400-1 in front of 14,265 spectators at Villa Park. Two goals from Gary Martindale gave Burscough victory against their better-fancied rivals, with Tamworth already celebrating the Dr Martens League Championship and promotion to the Nationwide Conference. The triumph was a dream return for Burscough's player-manager Shaun Teale, who spent six years with Aston Villa.

Tamworth started like favourites and were nearly ahead inside two minutes when the ball fell invitingly for Scott Rickards, but he headed over. Rickards was at the centre of much of Tamworth's attacking play and, when he laid the ball off, Richard Follett fired in a powerful shot that was deflected wide. Robinson was the next to receive from Rickards but after finding space in the area Burscough 'keeper Matt Taylor just managed to divert his effort into the side-netting.

Burscough did not threaten until the seventeenth minute when John Lawless unleashed an acrobatic volley from twenty-five yards that swerved past the post. Burscough began to find their discipline at the back and Tamworth found chances harder to come by. They were not helped by an injury to Rickards, who had to leave the field after being the victim of a crunching challenge. He eventually limped back on but his influence was not the same.

Burscough were coming more into the game and took the lead on twenty-five minutes with a superbly executed goal. John Lawless' pass ran nicely into the path of the onrushing Martindale and, with his colleague Peter Wright confusing the defence, Martindale was in the clear to strike the ball firmly into the net past the advancing Tamworth 'keeper Darren Acton. Tamworth responded immediately by gaining a free-kick thirty yards out, from which Mark Cooper's shot looked goal bound but was superbly stopped by the agility of Taylor pushing the ball over the bar to his left.

An early onslaught was expected from Tamworth at the start of the second half, but it was Burscough who were still looking the more dangerous and won a corner from which Ryan Bowen hit a first-time volley just wide from twenty yards. On fifty-five minutes Burscough were in dreamland. John Lawless advanced with the ball down the middle and from twenty-five yards struck a low shot that Acton could only push out into the path of Martindale, who drilled the ball past the helpless 'keeper. It capped an extraordinary performance from Martindale, who had to take a series of anti-inflammatory tablets and painkillers hours before the kick-off.

Tamworth replied with a free-kick which flew just over the bar and then a delightful move between Carl Macauley and Mark Byrne ended with the latter's shot from a difficult angle pushed away for a corner by Acton.

Tamworth would not lie down and with eleven minutes remaining they set up a grandstand finish. Warner latched onto a clearance and Cooper got on the end of his cross to poke past Taylor, despite Teale's desperate attempt to clear.

Burscough were forced onto the back foot, but Teale and Joe Taylor, who had been a tower of strength all afternoon, were in no mood to concede another and repelled a series of long balls. Tamworth became exposed at the back as they took more risks and on ninety minutes Paul Burns had the ball in the net for Burscough, but it was disallowed for an earlier foul. Peter Wright then broke away down the right and homed in on goal, but his shot hit the side netting.

Tamworth forced a corner in injury time, from which a resulting scramble provided a few suitably heart-stopping moments, until the ball was cleared into touch. Referee Uriah Rennie blew for time, and it was celebration time for Burscough.

Martindale later paid tribute to Teale for a rousing half-time team talk that inspired Burscough on their last leg towards trophy glory. 'I remember it clearly', he said. 'Shaun said: "Even if we have to dig a trench on our eighteen-yard line and defend, we will not get beaten". It was brilliant and really inspired us to go out there and finish the job. Shaun's got such a presence on the pitch and around the club. If you didn't know his age you would guess that he was twenty-five and not thirty-nine.'

Burscough came home to a heroes' welcome that stunned club secretary Stan Strickland. He said:

The scale of what we achieved only really sank in when we got home and saw the scenes at our ground. We were open mouthed with amazement at the sight of 2,000 people waiting to welcome us. It took us twenty minutes to complete the last thirty yards to the ground. For a village of our size to win the FA Trophy, after playing 12 games along the way, must rank up there with some of the greatest footballing achievements of all time.

However, the Burscough fairytale reached a sour conclusion when Teale was sacked at the end of June 2003 following a fall-out with the club's directors and the side began 2003/04 in a state of disarray.

Burscough: M. Taylor, Teale, J. Taylor, MacAuley, Lawless, Bowen, Wright, Norman, Martindale, Byrne, Burns. Substitutes: Bluck, McHale, Gary Maguire, Molineux, M. White.

Tamworth: Acton, Warner, Follett, Robinson, Walsh, Cooper, Colley, Evans, Rickards, McGorry, Sale. Substitutes: Hallam, Turner, Grocutt, Hatton, Barnes.

In Focus
Teale's Triumph

Shaun Teale was in all certainty the central figure behind Burscough's FA Trophy success. The Burscough player-manager returned in triumph to Villa Park, where he experienced the highlights of his career after joining Aston Villa for £300,000 from Bournemouth in 1989. But, despite winning the League Cup with Villa and helping them to a Premiership runners-up spot, Teale ranked Burscough's victory alongside the best. 'Without doubt, it easily ranks alongside everything else I've achieved in my professional playing career,' he said.

The reason for that lies in Burscough winning non-League's premier cup competition despite meagre resources that mean they are not even eligible for Conference status. 'To win a competition like the trophy on Burscough's resources is an incredible achievement', Teale explained. 'In a sense we are playing league matches for nothing, as the only thing we need to do is avoid relegation – we can't even be promoted.'

It was Teale who inspired Burscough to a sensational victory over eventual Conference Champions Yeovil, before netting the decisive penalty in the semi-final against Aylesbury United. The game was heading towards extra time when the spot kick was awarded and it needed nerves of steel to convert it.

Enter Teale, who was unruffled by the situation. He said, 'I knew it was all over then, because when we get a penalty, I never miss. Once I put the ball on the spot, I never look at the 'keeper. I walk away, make my mind up and do no turn until the whistle goes.' Teale smacked his spot kick straight down the middle to send Burscough to Villa Park. Teale, in his first season of management with Burscough, a club he played for as a seventeen-year-old, revelled in the responsibility. 'I knew that if I was to succeed as a manager I had to do things all my own way', he said. 'It helped my playing, as I find it easier to control things by being out on the pitch and the players seem to respond to me more than when I am stuck in the dugout.'

Routes to the Final

Burscough

First round	Burscough 0, Marine 0
First-round replay	Marine 1, Burscough 3
Second round	Harrogate Town 2, Burscough 2
Second-round replay	Burscough 3, Harrogate Town 2
Third round	Ilkestown Town 0, Burscough 3
Fourth round	Alfreton Town 1, Burscough 1
Fourth-round replay	Burscough 2, Alfreton Town 0
Fifth round	Burscough 5, Wakefield & Emley 0
Sixth round	Yeovil Town 0, Burscough 2
Semi-final, first leg	Aylesbury United 1, Burscough 1
Semi-final, second leg	Burscough 1, Aylesbury United 0

Tamworth

Second round	Tamworth 4, Accrington Stanley 1
Third round	Tamworth 3, Nuneaton Borough 0
Fourth round	Tamworth 3, Stevenage Borough 0
Fifth round	Margate 0, Tamworth 2
Sixth round	Farnborough Town 1, Tamworth 2
Semi-final, first leg	Tamworth 1, Havant & Waterlooville 0
Semi-final, second leg	Havant & Waterlooville 1, Tamworth 1

Above: Burscough's squad suited up before their big day at Villa Park.

Opposite: Burscough's Gary Martindale runs towards supporters after scoring the opening goal.

Right: Burscough player-manager Shaun Teale and skipper Carl Macauley hold the FA Trophy aloft.

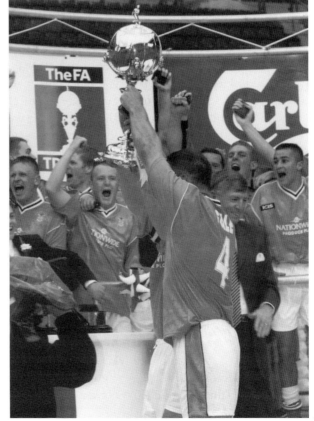

FA Trophy– Results of the Finals 1970-2003

1970	Macclesfield Town	2-0	Telford United	28,000
1971	Telford United	3-2	Hillingdon Borough	29,500
1972	Stafford Rangers	3-0	Barnet	24,000
1973	Scarborough	2-1 aet	Wigan Athletic	23,000
1974	Morecambe	2-1	Dartford	19,000
1975	Matlock Town	4-0	Scarborough	21,000
1976	Scarborough	3-2 aet	Stafford Rangers	21,000
1977	Scarborough	2-1	Dagenham	20,500
1978	Altrincham	3-1	Leatherhead	20,000
1979	Stafford Rangers	2-0	Kettering Town	32,000
1980	Dagenham	2-1	Mossley	26,000
1981	Bishop's Stortford	1-0	Sutton United	22,578
1982	Enfield	1-0	Altrincham	18,678
1983	Telford United	2-1	Northwich Victoria	22,071
1984	Northwich Victoria	1-1 2-1	Bangor City	14,200/5,805
1985	Wealdstone	2-1	Boston United	20,775
1986	Altrincham	1-0	Runcorn	15,700
1987	Kidderminster Harriers	0-0 2-1	Burton Albion	23,617/15,685
1988	Enfield	0-0 3-2	Telford United	21,328/7,005
1989	Telford United	1-0	Macclesfield Town	19,576
1990	Barrow	3-0	Leek Town	21,492
1991	Wycombe Wanderers	2-1	Kidderminster Harriers	34,842
1992	Colchester United	3-1	Witton Albion	32,254
1993	Wycombe Wanderers	4-1	Runcorn	32,968
1994	Woking	2-1	Runcorn	15,818
1995	Woking	2-1 aet	Kidderminster Harriers	17,815
1996	Macclesfield Town	3-1	Northwich Victoria	8,672
1997	Woking	1-0 aet	Dagenham & Redbridge	24,376
1998	Cheltenham Town	1-0	Southport	26,837
1999	Kingstonian	1-0	Forest Green Rovers	20,037
2000	Kingstonian	3-2	Kettering Town	20,034
2001	Canvey Island	1-0	Forest Green Rovers	10,007
2002	Yeovil Town	2-0	Stevenage Borough	18,809
2003	Burscough	2-1	Tamworth	14,265

Summary of Winners

3
Scarborough, Telford United, Woking

2
Altrincham, Enfield, Kingstonian, Macclesfield Town, Stafford Rangers, Wycombe Wanderers

1
Barrow, Bishop's Stortford, Burscough, Canvey Island, Cheltenham Town, Colchester United, Dagenham, Kidderminster Harriers, Matlock Town, Morecambe, Northwich Victoria, Wealdstone, Yeovil Town

Also from Tempus Publishing

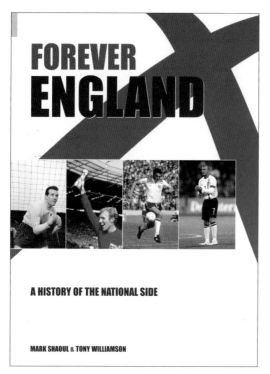

Forever England
The History of the National Side
MARK SHAOUL & TONY WILLIAMSON

The definitive history of the English national side

From the days of the amateur gentlemen of the 1870s to the present day, *Forever England* is an insightful and fascinating account of the history of the country's national football team. England's finest hour in 1966 is covered in detail, as are the other highs and lows of 130 years of international competition. The book also covers the careers of England's all-time greats and is an essential read for everyone who is interested in the history of the Three Lions. The enthralling narrative, which includes England team line-ups for key games, match reports and every group table involving England from all major tournaments, is supported by 200 illustrations.

0 7524 2939 6

If you are interested in purchasing other books published by Tempus,
or in case you have difficulty finding any Tempus books in your local bookshop,
you can also place orders directly through our website
www.tempus-publishing.com
or from
BOOKPOST, Freepost, PO Box 29, Douglas, Isle of Man IM99 1BQ
Tel 01624 836000   email bookshop@enterprise.net